CHRISTIAN
PRAYER
FOR TODAY

Also available in the For Today series:

CHRISTIAN
PRAYER
FOR TODAY

Martha L. Moore-Keish

WJK WESTMINSTER
JOHN KNOX PRESS
LOUISVILLE · KENTUCKY

Book design by Sharon Adams
Cover design by Eric Walljasper, Minneapolis, MN

First edition
Published by Westminster John Knox Press
Louisville, Kentucky

This book is printed on acid-free paper that meets the American National Standards Institute Z39.48 standard. ∞

PRINTED IN THE UNITED STATES OF AMERICA

09 10 11 12 13 14 15 16 17 18 — 10 9 8 7 6 5 4 3 2 1

Library of Congress Cataloging-in-Publication Data

Moore-Keish, Martha L.
    Christian prayer for today / Martha L. Moore-Keish.
        p. cm. — (For today series)
    Includes bibliographical references.
    ISBN 978-0-664-23074-6 (alk. paper)
    1. Prayer—Christianity.   I. Title.
    BV210.3.M67   2009
    248.3'2—dc22
                                        2008028013

Contents

Series Introduction

*T*he For Today series is intended to provide reliable and accessible resources for the study of important biblical texts, theological documents, and Christian practices. The series is written by experts who are committed to making the results of their studies available to those with no particular biblical or theological training. The goal is to provide an engaging means to study texts and practices that are familiar to laity in churches. The authors are all committed to the importance of their topics and to communicating the significance of their understandings to a wide audience. The emphasis is not only on what these subjects have meant in the past, but also their value in the present—"For Today."

Our hope is that the books in this series will find eager readers in churches, particularly in the context of education classes. The authors are educators and pastors who wish to engage church laity in the issues raised by their topics. They seek to provide guidance for learning, for nurture, and for growth in Christian experience.

To enhance the educational usefulness of these volumes, Questions for Discussion are included at the end of each chapter.

We hope the books in this series will be important resources to enhance Christian faith and life.

The Publisher

Introduction

*A*round the dinner table a family joins hands. For a moment, before plunging into pasta and salad and news of the day, they look at one another. Then the youngest child begins to sing, "The Lord be with you. . . ."

In a dimly lit corner of St. Anthony's Church, a woman lights a candle before the image of the Madonna. For a few moments she stands gazing at the image of mother and child, wordlessly aching to understand her distant teenage son.

Beside a hospital bed a man watches helplessly as his best friend struggles to hold onto life after years of devastating illness. Grasping his friend's hand, he whispers to the heart monitor, "Jesus, please don't let him go yet."

The reporter on the battlefield looks around at the mutilated bodies of victims of a bomb blast and cries out, "Why, God? Why couldn't you stop this from happening?"

On Sunday morning, members of First Church remain gathered around the table at the end of the Communion service. Together they recite the familiar words, "Bless the Lord, my soul, and bless God's holy name; bless the Lord, my soul, and forget not all God's benefits."

Each of these events is prayer. In a variety of ways, the people in these scenes are all reaching out beyond themselves: giving thanks, asking for help, weeping in despair, crying out in anguish. Some use words and some do not; some seem to expect a response while others clearly do not. Perhaps some do not even think that they are praying. In each case, however, a person or a group of people is seeking or acknowledging or hoping for a dimension of reality more profound than their senses alone will admit. Countless events like these occur each day around the world. The very fact that we recognize these scenes and can imagine many more is enough, for now, to begin a conversation about prayer.

What is prayer? What happens when we pray? Does it affect God? Does it affect us? What is *Christian* prayer in particular? How do we pray? These are the major questions this book will address. Along the way we will reflect on tricky topics like what it means to pray in the name of Jesus, what constitutes answered prayer, and whether you ought to pray for parking spaces.

Before we can think about prayer directly, however, it helps to think about who is involved in prayer: God and ourselves. Who are we, and who is the God to, with, and in whom we pray? Starting with the question of *who* will help us think more adequately about the *what* and *how* of prayer. Indeed, whether or not we acknowledge it, each time we come to prayer, we do so with some notion of the character of the One to whom we pray, and some presupposition about the character of ourselves, the pray-ers. For instance, if we think of God primarily as an all-powerful king and ourselves as humble servants, this understanding will likely give rise to prayers like "O Lord, I am your servant; I am your servant, the child of your serving girl. You have loosed my bonds. . . . I will pay my vows to the Lord in the presence of all his people, in the courts of the house of the Lord, in your midst, O Jerusalem" (Ps. 116:16, 18–19). If we think of God as the creative source of all things and the power that animates all of life, then our prayers might sound more like this: "O Lord, how manifold are your works! In wisdom you have made them all; the earth is full of your creatures. . . . [W]hen you take away their breath, they die and return to their dust. When you send forth your spirit, they are created; and you renew the face of the ground" (Ps. 104:24, 29–30). Our approach to prayer depends in part on whether we understand God to be distant or near, profoundly other or profoundly intimate to our being.

Our understanding of God and of ourselves fundamentally shapes our understanding of the relationship between God and ourselves, a relationship that is enacted in prayer. Beginning with attention to God, therefore—guided by Scripture and tradition and accompanied by deep attention to our own life in God—can enable us to understand and enter more fully into truly Christian prayer.

Every theological essay is shaped by the particular history of the writer. My own reflections on prayer arise from the convergence of several streams: lifelong Presbyterian formation and Reformed theological education, profound interest in interreligious conversation, commitment to ecumenical dialogue, and deep respect for classical liturgical practices. In the Presbyterian congregation where I was raised, I learned the skills of stilling my body, paying attention, listening—all important virtues when it comes to the practice of prayer. From that community I also absorbed the rhythms of carefully crafted public prayer and the power of congregational singing as a form of praying.

As I grew up, I became curious as well about the prayer practices of other religious traditions, especially Buddhism and Hinduism. I read books on Zen and experimented with meditation on the gold shag carpet of my bedroom. I went off to college and learned about the devotional practices of Hindu pilgrims. After college, I lived in India and observed firsthand the vivid, embodied prayer practices of popular devotion: shrines in homes, sacrifices in the temples, pilgrimages to the Ganges. I returned to my country and my church newly attentive to the ways the body is involved in prayer, and to patterns of both public and private ritual behavior.

These questions led me to study Christian liturgical practices, with an eye to how worship both reflects and shapes patterns of believing. As I learned more about Christian liturgical history, I came to love the ancient ways of praying that have been recovered by many churches in the past half-century. I learned to pray using patterns shared by Christians across the centuries and across the world. Liturgical study flowed naturally into ecumenical dialogue, an endeavor that has exposed me to yet more varieties of Christian praying. Through involvement in ecumenical dialogue, I continue to seek understanding of the genuine differences among Christians, even as I also affirm that we all offer prayers to the same triune God.

I write this book not as an expert on prayer, but as one who is still learning to pray. This is the invitation I now extend to you. Ultimately, these theological reflections on prayer are intended to invite you more deeply into the practice of prayer itself. For some, years of praying prompt questions about what is going on. For others, it is difficult even to enter into the practice of prayer without some conceptual map of what is happening in that event. That is to say, some people begin with doing and then move to reflection, while others begin with theological reflection and then move into practice. In both cases, practice and reflection inform one another. No matter where you are beginning, this book tries to provide a way of thinking about prayer that can lead into a new or renewed practical life of prayer.

This book is for anyone who has wondered about God or about the practice of Christian prayer. If you have found yourself thinking from time to time about what it means to pray, about whether anything really happens in prayer, about why or whether God listens to the petitions and what we ought or ought not to say in prayer, then welcome to the conversation.

Questions for Discussion

1. How do you describe prayer?
2. How do you think about God when you pray? As near or far away? Familiar or unfamiliar?
3. What experiences in your life have shaped the ways you pray?

1

Who Is the God We Encounter in Prayer?

O Lord, open my lips. And my mouth shall proclaim your praise.
—Based on Psalm 51:15, *Book of Common Worship*

With these words has morning prayer begun in monasteries across the Western church since the early Middle Ages, and so begins morning prayer today in Roman Catholic and Episcopalian, Lutheran, Presbyterian, and other Protestant churches, and for all those peculiar individuals who use the ancient order. "O Lord, open my lips." This prayer, with its origins in the prayer life of the people of Israel, is particularly powerful when these are the first words of the day, after keeping silence for the night (whether in a monastery or family home). These words acknowledge that God both gives and receives our words, both empowers our prayers and is the goal of our prayers. This simple response, echoed around the world and across the centuries of Christian worship, leads us into the complex mystery of the God to, with, and in whom we pray.

Where is God in this prayer? Quick reflection reveals that the "Lord" addressed here does not stand only in one place. The Lord is, first of all, the one whom we beg to open our lips. God enables speech in the first place, and thereby enables our praise. Without the activity of this Lord, there could be no praying at all. So this Lord-who-opens-lips is the God who creates all things, the one who forms humanity from the dust, who is the ultimate source of our being. This is the aspect of God whom Christian theology has classically named "Father," the first person of the Trinity.

/ 1

The Trinity?

The subject of the Trinity often elicits strong reactions from Christians and non-Christians alike. Some Muslims take real offense at the notion that God is "three in one," since a bedrock affirmation of Islam is the oneness of God. I have heard that in some areas of the Muslim world, popular bumper stickers declare, "The Lord is ONE Lord," to distinguish Islamic monotheism from Christian Trinitarian faith. Our Jewish brothers and sisters similarly object to the paradox of the Trinity, because of the basic affirmation of Scripture: "Hear, O Israel: the LORD is our God, the LORD alone" (Deut. 6:4). In this age of religious pluralism, we need to acknowledge frankly that the Trinity poses a particular challenge for some interreligious relationships.

Even among Christians, discussion of the Trinity often raises concerns, either because it uses nonbiblical terminology, or because it depends on patriarchal male language, or because it is simply impossible to comprehend. All of these are serious and complex questions that merit careful attention. Yet the doctrine of the Trinity, for all of its difficulties, can point toward the mystery of the God we encounter in prayer: a God who is simultaneously the source of our prayers, the one who hears and responds to our prayers, and the one who stands beside us in praying.

The doctrine of the Trinity developed gradually over the first few centuries of Christian history. In the fourth century, there emerged an ecumenical consensus that God is "one in essence, distinguished in three persons." When we hear this language of "person" today, we usually think of a self-contained individual who has a body and a mind and acts independently of others. However, at the time that this language developed, "person" (*persona* in Latin) had a very different meaning. It meant something more like "role," like a character in a drama. This language offered a way of naming the Christian conviction that the God encountered in Jesus Christ was the same God encountered at Sinai and at Pentecost. This God, the church stammered, was not simply *one* but was also somehow *three*. To worship "God in three persons, blessed Trinity" is not to worship a divine committee, a holy three-member board of directors who reside in heaven and make all decisions concerning creation. Rather, to say that God is "three persons" is to point toward the inexpressible mystery that the one God encounters us in a variety of ways:

- as the source of our being, who made covenant with the people of Israel, delivered them from slavery in Egypt and from exile in Babylon;
- as Jesus the Christ, who taught and healed, was tortured and murdered, and then rose from the dead; and
- as the mysterious power who animates the church and the lives of individual believers around the world even now.

So to speak of God in "three persons" is an invitation to encounter the Holy Mystery in prayer in three dimensions.

Source of Prayer

O Lord, open my lips. This simple request first calls to mind the story of creation, in which the Holy One shaped humanity out of the dust of the earth and breathed life into our bodies. "Open my lips" voices our utter dependence on the prior activity of the One who made us. Our lips cannot move until they are opened by our Creator. As the psalmist says, "When you send forth your spirit, they are created; and you renew the face of the ground" (Ps. 104:30). The Lord opens our lips, in the first place, in the very moment of our creation.

Yet there is more: the prayer for God to open our lips recalls also the story of Isaiah's vision of "the Lord sitting on a throne, high and lofty" (Isa. 6:1). In that passage, the prophet marvels at the majesty of the Lord and at the seraphs who surround him, and in response he calls out, "Woe is me! I am lost, for I am a man of unclean lips, and I live among a people of unclean lips." At that moment one of the seraphs flies to him with a live coal from the altar, touches his lips, and says, "Now that this has touched your lips, your guilt has departed and your sin is blotted out." Having been cleansed in this way, the prophet is sent to proclaim the word of the Lord to the people.

Remembering Isaiah's vision, we can hear the petition "open my lips" in another way. These words evoke not only our utter dependence on God our Creator, the source of all words, but also our dependence on God who purifies and forgives us for all of our wrong words. We are able to pray at all because God creates our lips, and we are able to proclaim and pray rightly because God cleanses our lips. In the next chapter, I will talk about sin, or separation from God, as a basic dimension of human existence. We do not live, or love, or even pray as we ought. But God reaches out over the divide and touches our lips, so that even our awkward mumblings can be heard as songs of praise. Any prayer that we offer is possible only because we are both created *and cleansed* by the one whom Jesus called Father, the maker of heaven and earth.

O Lord, open my lips. This simple prayer evokes God the Creator, the source of our being and the one who blots out our sin. Yet these words also call on the Spirit of God, the Holy Spirit, who empowers our praying. The Spirit is the life of God that invades our being. We might say that God the Father opens our lips "in the beginning," as the ultimate giver of life, while God the Spirit opens our lips more intimately, as the presence of God within us at each moment. God's Spirit gives life and continues to empower us as the breath beneath our breathing. This most intimate dimension of the triune God is another vital aspect of Christian praying.

Think about your own experiences of prayer. Perhaps there have been moments in your daily life when, unexpectedly, you remembered an old friend with a wave of gratitude. Perhaps you have thought of a distant acquaintance, with an urgent concern about that person's well-being. These are tiny eruptions of the Spirit's work within us, prompting us to prayer: "Thank you, gracious God." "Have mercy on her, Jesus." Such movement of the Spirit also pervades public worship any time people genuinely enter into prayer with and for others. "Thank you, gracious God." "Have mercy on them, Jesus." These words come from human impulse, to be sure, but such human impulse is deeply grounded in the impulse of the Spirit.

The presence of the holy is not only beyond us and before us but also deep within us. The very impulse to pray is of the Spirit. In prayer, God the Spirit opens our lips, speaking in and through our words. Paul the apostle affirms this when he says, "We do not know how to pray as we ought, but that very Spirit intercedes with sighs too deep for words. And God, who searches the heart, knows what is the mind of the Spirit, because the Spirit intercedes for the saints according to the will of God" (Rom. 8:26–27). As this passage attests, left to ourselves we do not know how to pray, and we pray badly, for the wrong things, using poor and clumsy speech. (More on that later.) Yet the good news that Paul offers here is the assurance that we are not alone in our prayers. When we pray, the Spirit works in and through us to make our prayers more adequate and bring them home to God.

John Calvin appealed to this passage from Romans to support his view that we only pray rightly because of the power of the Spirit. God gives us the Spirit as a "teacher in prayer." However, Calvin cautions, "these things are not said in order that we, favoring our own slothfulness, may give over the function of prayer to the Spirit of God, and vegetate in that carelessness to which we are all too prone."[1] Rather, we should actively seek the Spirit's guidance in prayer and give thanks that God helps us in this way. The wonder of prayer, when we think about it, is that in the very act of praying itself, God is with us. God does not simply wait for us to get the words right before deigning to listen. God inspires the prayers themselves, graciously leaning into our hearts so that God speaks to God through us. This means that we need to seek the Spirit's guidance, but also offer thanks for the very gift of prayer at all.

In all of these ways, as Creator, cleanser, and empowering Spirit, God is the source of our praying. God opens our lips both ultimately and intimately, inviting us into holy encounter.

The One Who Hears Prayer

O Lord, open my lips. And my mouth shall proclaim your praise. Who is this God, this "Lord" named in prayer? So far, this little responsive verse has led us to say that God as Creator and as Spirit both encourages and enables us to pray in the first place. Yet this is not the only way we encounter God in the context of this prayer. Listen again to the words and notice where God is: God opens the lips of the psalmist, and God also receives the praise from the lips that are opened. God precedes the prayer, and God receives the prayer.

For those who delight in wordplay, we might say that God is *before* our prayer in two different senses. Before we speak at all, God enables us to pray, so God is before us in time. But further, as the one to whom we pray, God is before us as the audience of our prayers. God is before us as beginning, and God is before us as our end.

One fancy way that theologians speak about this is to say that God is both *source* and *telos* (end or goal). God is the one who gives life to all things, and God is the one toward whom the whole creation moves. All things have their origin in God, and all things are intended to find their fulfillment in God. As source of all things, God shines like light, overflows like water, in the act of creation. Creation, then, reflects its source. Therefore, the end for which we are created is to reflect the glory of the one who created us. The Westminster Shorter Catechism begins by asking, "What is our chief end?" What are we (human beings) made for? The answer is: we are made to glorify and enjoy God forever.[2] We are created to return to God the glory that was poured out in creation itself. Prayer is a primary mode of glorifying and enjoying God. Just as God is the source and telos of all things, so also God is the source and telos of prayer.

But it is not enough to say simply that God is an audience before us, receiving any random form of address. Once the lips are opened, they utter *praise*! What does this suggest? That the One to whom prayers are offered draws a response of adoration. In other words, this Lord is *good*. Otherwise, why would the psalmist sing out praise?

Jesus' words in Luke 11:1–13 illuminate the basic goodness of God to whom we pray. At the beginning of the passage, the disciples come to Jesus and ask him, "Lord, teach us to pray." In response, he offers them one version of what we now call the Lord's Prayer. He follows that brief prayer with a set of parables about those who ask for and receive good gifts, first from a friend awakened in the night, and then from a father. Prayer, he suggests, is like asking a friend or a father for what we need. Jesus concludes the passage by saying, "If you, then, who are evil, know how to give good gifts to your children, how much more will the heavenly Father give the Holy Spirit to those who ask him!" (v. 13).

When we pray, according to Jesus, we pray to one who loves us and cares for us just as a father cares for his children. Therefore, we pray in confidence, like a child asking a parent for what she needs, or asking to be forgiven for misbehavior, or asking to be protected from the terrors of the night. The disciples beg, "Lord, teach us to pray." Jesus does give the disciples a set prayer, and the church has faithfully repeated this prayer over the centuries as we come together to worship God. But more than a form of prayer, Jesus teaches about the nature of the God to whom we pray. God is like a generous father, Jesus says. God does not stay in bed when his children are hungry outside. God does not play practical jokes on us, giving scorpions instead of eggs. God stands ready and waiting to feed, forgive, and shelter us—and more, God stands ready and waiting to feed, forgive, and shelter all the children of the world. In other words, God hears our prayers and answers them, desiring to give good gifts to his children.

O Lord, open my lips, and my mouth shall proclaim your praise. Entering into this prayer draws our attention to the source of praying, which is at once God our Creator and the life-breath of the Holy Spirit within us. It also directs our attention to the recipient of praise, God our loving parent who is worthy of our prayers, who listens to and desires the petitions of our hearts and minds. So just in the space of twelve words, we encounter God as beginning and ending, as deep source and ultimate end of our praying.

Companion in Prayer

Yet even this summary does not exhaust the presence of God in this brief prayer. What if we step back and ask whose words these are that we are praying? *O Lord, open my lips. And my mouth shall proclaim your praise.* These are human words, certainly, words that Christians can and have voiced for centuries. Yet is this simply our voice praying these words?

In 1938, German pastor and teacher Dietrich Bonhoeffer challenged his community to think about prayer, and particularly praying the Psalms, in another way. He suggested that the Psalms teach us to pray, and that when we encounter psalms that are difficult for us, we come to realize that someone else is praying, not us. In giving voice to the word of God in the Psalms, we come to realize that the Word of God is praying in and through us.[3] So then, when we pray, "O Lord, open lips, and my mouth shall proclaim your praise," the words themselves are those of Christ, and of Christ's body, the church.

If this sounds strange, think about it this way. The Psalms were Jesus' own prayer book, the expressions of praise and lament and anger and thanksgiving that shaped the prayer life of the Jewish community in Jesus' time. We can see the influence of the Psalms on Jesus' speech as recorded in the Gospels. For instance, when Jesus proclaims in his Sermon on the Mount, "Blessed are the meek, for they will inherit the earth" (Matt. 5:5), he surely echoes Psalm 37:11: "the meek shall inherit the land, and delight themselves in abundant prosperity." In Luke 20:42, Jesus explicitly cites Psalm 110:1: "The Lord said to my Lord, 'Sit at my right hand, until I make your enemies your footstool.'" And scholars have long recognized that when Jesus cries out from the cross "Eli, Eli, lema sabachthani?"—"My God, my God, why have you forsaken me?"—(Matt. 27:46), he is using the words of lament from the opening of Psalm 22. Even beyond these specific examples, we know that the psalms played a major role in the liturgical life of Jewish synagogues in the first century. Jesus learned to pray using the words of the Psalms. This means that when we use the Psalms in prayer, we are truly praying in the voice of Christ.

Furthermore, following Jesus, the Christian church has relied on the Psalms as the foundation of prayer since its earliest days. The writer of Ephesians alludes to this, calling the community to "be filled with the Spirit, as you sing psalms and hymns and spiritual songs among yourselves" (Eph. 5:18b–19). So also the writer of Colossians exhorts the church to "sing psalms, hymns, and spiritual songs to God" (Col. 3:16). The Psalms have formed the backbone of daily prayer services for Christian communities for as long as there is historical evidence. So when we pray the Psalms, we are not offering up simply our own words, but we are praying in the voice of Jesus and of the whole church.

Though this is clearly true when we pray the Psalms, it is true in some measure each time Christians pray. When we offer up words of prayer to God, these words are always formed by Christ and the church, who have taught us to pray. This does not mean that we simply parrot the words we have been given. It does not mean that these are not truly our own prayers. It does mean that when Christians offer prayers, we do so in community with Christ and Christ's body, the church. And more, when Christians offer prayers, Christ is praying through us and with us. In this way, Christ is our companion in prayer.

The Reformed Protestant tradition has often summed up Christ's work by calling him Mediator. Jesus Christ stands in the middle between us and God, fully human and fully divine, representing each party to the other (much the way contemporary mediators do today). This understanding of Christ as Mediator can help us to think about Christ's companionship in prayer. As human, Jesus shows us how we are to pray, giving us model words and pointing our attention to God's goodness. He gives us the example of true human prayer that we are to imitate. As God incarnate, Jesus Christ shows us the ways of God to whom we pray. He reveals that God is one who desires intimate relationship with us, condescending even to become one of us. Jesus shows us in the flesh our God, who "casts down the mighty" and "sends the rich empty away" but who is also "slow to anger, and abounding in steadfast love." He embodies at one and the same time true humanity and true divinity, bringing the two into communion with each other.

O Lord, open my lips, and my mouth shall proclaim your praise. If we turn back to the little verse we have been considering in this chapter, hearing it as the voice of Jesus Christ, this opens up yet another dimension of what is going on in prayer. Here, Christ models the appropriate human relationship to God: dependence on God for creation, cleansing, and empowerment, and praise of God's goodness. At the same time, Christ reveals to us the God who is worthy of praise.

But there is one more thing to notice, if we hear these words as a prayer of Christ our companion. If Jesus himself prays, "O Lord, open my lips, and my mouth shall proclaim your praise," then this illumines the relationship between Jesus and the one he calls "Lord" and "Father." And if Jesus Christ is not only a real human but also God incarnate, then what we are witnessing is a relationship within the heart of the triune God. Jesus Christ, the Son of God, speaks here to God the Father, the source of being. Through these words in the mouth of Christ, we may see a tiny glimpse of the relational mystery of the Trinity. In prayer, through Christ, we also enter into that relationship, into that holy communion.

Conclusion: Prayer as Participation in God

If you have read carefully, you may have noticed that the three ways I have described God in this chapter do not correspond exactly to the three classical persons of the Trinity. Ruminating on an ancient prayer text has led me instead to reflections on God as source of prayer, as object (or recipient) of prayer, and as companion in prayer. These terms are not intended to replace the classical Trinitarian formulation of "Father, Son, and Holy Spirit." Rather, describing God as source, object, and companion in prayer is an attempt to name the ways that the Holy Trinity really encounters us as we pray.

My own reflections on the Trinity and prayer are similar, though not identical, to those of C. S. Lewis in *Mere Christianity*. He describes prayer as being "drawn into that three-personal life":

> An ordinary simple Christian kneels down to say his prayers. He is trying to get in touch with God. But if a Christian, he knows that what is prompting him to pray is also God: God, so to speak, inside him. But he also knows that all his real knowledge of God comes through Christ, the Man who was God—that Christ is standing beside him, helping him to pray, praying for him. You see what is happening. God is the thing to which he is praying— the goal he is trying to reach. God is also the thing inside him which is pushing him on—the motive power. God is also the road or bridge along which he is being pushed to that goal. So that the whole threefold life of the three-personal being is actually going on in that ordinary little bedroom where an ordinary Christian is saying his prayers.[4]

Lewis speaks of God as goal, "motive power," and road or bridge, while I have used language of God as source, object, and companion. Yet we end up with much the same affirmation: that prayer itself, rightly understood, is an entrance into the Trinitarian life of God.

As we see most clearly in Jesus' own example of prayer, one distinctive feature of Christian praying is entering into the relationship between Jesus and the one he calls "Abba, Father." In later chapters, we will focus on what it means to pray in the name of Jesus, and what constitutes distinctively Christian prayer, but here we have an initial clue to both of these questions. Jesus Christ, fully human, knows the full range of human experience: joy, laughter, grief, suffering, death. He is one of us. Jesus Christ, fully divine, also knows the depth of God's eternal love. He is one with God. Jesus shows us that God's very being is not solitary but consists of divine community. This is what the doctrine of the Trinity tries to announce: that God is love within God's own being. Within the heart of God there is a joyous dance of communion among three "persons" who delight in each other and pour themselves out for one another.

God is holy communion within God's own self. In Christ, we glimpse this communion in the heart of God, and we also realize that this holy One-in-Three seeks communion with us. In prayer, we enter into this communion, as we acknowledge that God is at once the source of our prayer, the one to whom we pray, and our companion in prayer. When we turn to prayer, before we even open our lips, we are surrounded and suffused by the mystery of the Holy Trinity.

Who is the God we encounter in prayer? God is source, goal, and companion in prayer, the Holy Trinity that envelops us as we pray, drawing us (if we open ourselves to it) into ever deeper communion with God. True prayer is thus participation in God.

Questions for Discussion

1. Where do you imagine God when you pray? Ahead of you? Beside you? Within you?
2. How does the understanding of God as Trinity affect your praying?
3. What do you think of Dietrich Bonhoeffer's suggestion that when we pray the Psalms, we are praying in the voice of Christ?

Who Are We Who Pray?

As a deer longs for flowing streams,
  so my soul longs for you, O God.
My soul thirsts for God,
  for the living God.

—Psalm 42:1-2a

*C*hapter 1 explored the question "Who is the God we encounter in prayer?" Reflection on Psalm 51:15 led us to consider God as at once source of prayer, goal of prayer, and companion in prayer. In praying, we are surrounded by holy triune mystery. In this chapter we turn to the other partner in prayer, namely, ourselves. Who are we human beings who pray?

Psalm 42 eloquently combines prayer to God and internal dialogue with the soul. This ancient aching song offers one rich portrait of what it means to be a praying human. In this chapter, I will trace the movement of this psalm as it meditates on human longing, memory, and hope. These different angles can help us to glimpse some of the complexity about the human condition in relation to God.

Longing for God

The opening verses of this psalm cry out in anguish, voicing the acute pain of separation from God:

As a deer longs for flowing streams,
  so my soul longs for you, O God.

> My soul thirsts for God,
>   for the living God.
> When shall I come and behold
>   the face of God?
> My tears have been my food
>   day and night,
> while people say to me continually,
>   "Where is your God?"
>   (Ps. 42:1–3)

Have you ever woken up to this kind of longing, this kind of near-physical ache to know God's presence? Have you heard these words of the psalmist with a pang of recognition? The words of the psalmist here are surely voicing the pain of a particular people at a particular point in history, and we cannot overlook the specific circumstances that gave rise to this lament. Yet the ache of separation from God "as a deer longs for flowing streams" has resonated through the lives of Jewish and Christian worshipers for thousands of years. The psalm does not present a situation that is unique to the writer; rather, long ing is a basic dimension of human life. In particular, the opening of this psalm shows us three things about the human condition:

- We are separated from God.
- We depend on God.
- We desire closer relationship with God.

At first, the psalmist portrays estrangement from God as profoundly painful as the thirst of an animal who cannot find enough water. Anyone who has suffered dehydration knows the experience that the writer is describing here. Without sufficient water, we grow weak, dizzy, and disoriented. So too the psalmist voices a kind of dizziness and disorientation. He aches, longs, pants for God, who seems to be absent. *When shall I come and behold the face of God?* The psalm has endured so long because this very condition of longing has been familiar to people through the centuries.

Not all people are aware of a deep longing for God. Yet we have all known moments when the everyday tasks of our lives are suddenly unsatisfying, when our most intimate relationships flounder with petty arguments and misunderstandings, when we turn around and discover that the goals we worked so hard to achieve do not bring lasting happiness. The fragility of life, its temporary pleasures and limited achievements, leads all of us to disappointment at some point in our lives. In these moments, we cry out for something more permanent, a more lasting joy, a deeper knowledge of something real and authentic. This reaching out for "something more" is, at its root, the longing of the heart for God.

In prayer we acknowledge that we long for God. Longing means that we are separated from God; the world as a whole and we as individuals are not completely at one with the One who created us. Living with this separation, this estrangement, is not the way we are supposed to be.

"Not the way we are supposed to be"—this is one way of talking about the condition that the Christian tradition has named "sin." This term "sin" has often been understood too narrowly to refer to particular acts of social transgression. In our day, sin is too often associated only with certain expressions of sexuality, or in popular culture, with overindulgence in food. (How many times have you heard a chocolate dessert described as "sinful"?) But it is helpful to pull back and regard sin as a more fundamental description of human alienation from God.

Sin may be expressed in a variety of ways, yet it is never exhausted by its particular expressions. Sexuality may indeed be expressed in sinful ways, for instance. So also consumption of food and drink, especially in our culture, may be an expression of sin. But sin is always more than particular acts. To say that we are "sinners" is simply to say that the world is not as it ought to be, and we are not as we ought to be. We live apart from God.

My soul thirsts for God, for the living God. These words capture the pain of separation. Yet they also point beyond that separation. All of the thirsty longing at the beginning of the psalm is not presented as the natural state of affairs. The psalmist cries out, "When shall I come and behold the face of God?" He reports that his enemies taunt him, "Where is your God?" These are not idle questions but cries that protest the absence of God as a condition contrary to the way things ought to be.

Go back to the opening verse of the psalm: "As a deer longs for flowing streams, so my soul longs for you, O God." This is a cry of separation, but it is also a declaration that humanity depends on God for life, just as animals depend on water. Human life cannot survive without water; so also, this psalm suggests, we cannot live without God. We are utterly dependent creatures, relying on our Maker for all that we have and all that we are.

In the first chapter, I suggested that the simple petition "O Lord, open my lips" calls us to recognize that God is the source of our praying. Before we even open our lips, God forms us and enables our lips to move. Psalm 42 also implies that God is our source and sustenance; our very lives depend on God. In chapter 1, I affirmed that God is the source of our being and source of our praying; here I am affirming the same thing from the human point of view: *we depend* on God to be the source of our being and source of our praying. We cannot do it alone.

My soul thirsts for God, for the living God. This leads to a further discovery about what it means to be human. The thirst, the desire to be with God, suggests that humanity, in the person of the psalmist, is intended for relationship with God. So we might say that the psalm points not only back, to the way we were created, and to the separation that we experience, but also ahead, to an anticipated future when we will be restored to God's presence. *When shall I come and behold the face of God?* We, like the psalmist, do not have the answer to this question. But notice that the psalmist does not ask, "*Shall* I come and behold the face of God?" The question is not whether he will be restored to God's presence, but when. Might this itself be a glimpse of hope in the midst of sadness, a flicker of confidence in the midst of desperate longing? We are made for communion with God, the psalmist seems to know. And we live in hope that someday that intention for who we are will be fulfilled.

When shall I come and behold the face of God? This psalm has already revealed some basic features of what it means to be human: we are alienated from God, and yet we are dependent on God for our lives, and we are made for communion with God. The tense interplay between these dimensions of human existence comes out in prayer. We thank God for our lives—and we beseech God to come into those areas of our lives that are most God-forsaken. We thank God for sustaining the beauty of the world—and we beseech God to heal those areas in the world that are most God-forsaken. We cannot live apart from

God—and yet we often live for long stretches without being able to sense God's presence.

How do we account for this tension we experience, between lament and thanksgiving, between the despairing ache over God's absence and the eager ache in anticipation of God's presence? Many theologians have talked about this as the tension between the false self, which imagines its own independence, and the true self, which is in relationship with God. Roman Catholic monk and theologian Thomas Merton, for instance, affirms that the true self is in union with God, while the false self imagines separation from God to be the way things really are. This is sin—imagining human independence as real.[1] Catholic theologian Karl Rahner speaks in similar terms, claiming that the "illusory I" that means only immediate consciousness is a recent invention. The "true I" is united with God in the depths of the human soul.[2]

Both Merton and Rahner help us to see that we humans live in a dilemma, on the one hand intimately related to God on whom we depend for our very lives, and on the other hand trying all the time to deny that life-giving relationship. We pretend that we are independent beings, that we can make it on our own, that we define ourselves and determine our own ways in the world. Yet no one, man or woman, is truly "self-made." When we acknowledge this, when we admit our dependence on God and realize our basic relationship to the One who gives us breath and life, then we come face to face with our truest selves. This is the self we try to nurture in prayer: the one who acknowledges and delights in communion with God. As C. S. Lewis puts it, "The prayer preceding all prayers is 'May it be the real I who speaks. May it be the real Thou that I speak to.'"[3]

Some Protestant theologians raise concerns about the language of the true self being "at one with God in the depths of the human soul," as Rahner puts it. This could sound like all we need to do is discover God at the depths of our being, rather than rely on God in Jesus Christ to reach out and save us. To some, this sounds like the effort is ours, rather than God's. Karl Barth, for instance, does not describe an already existing union with God that we simply need to discover and acknowledge. Yet in his own way, Barth plays a variation on this theme of the true and false self in prayer. He declares, "When we pray, our human condition is unveiled to us, and we know then that we are in that distress and also in that hope. It is God who places us in this situation; but at the same time he comes to our aid. Prayer is thus our human response when we understand our distress and know that help will come."[4] For Barth, too, prayer involves an "unveiling" of the true self, which knows its need and also knows that God will come to help.

My soul thirsts for God, for the living God. When shall I come and behold the face of God? The longing of the psalmist shows us something about the human condition: that we live as if we are separated from God, and yet that we depend deeply on God for our very lives. In prayer, we give voice to both of these aspects of ourselves, trying to peel back the layers of artifice that give the illusion of self-sufficiency.

Later in Psalm 42 the writer returns to the pain of separation from God:

> I say to God, my rock,
>   "Why have you forgotten me?
> Why must I walk about mournfully
>   because the enemy oppresses me?"
> As with a deadly wound in my body,
>   my adversaries taunt me,
> while they say to me continually,
>   "Where is your God?"
>
>   (vv. 9–10)

While we have heard already the lament about God's apparent absence, the psalmist now adds the further dimension of the taunting of enemies. This suggests that we are intended not only for communion with God but also for community with others—yet we do not live out this community with others as we ought. We oppress, taunt, and wound one another. There is a deep connection here between the alienation of the self from God and the alienation from other people. When God seems to have forgotten the people, human oppression and humiliation grow stronger. Sin, as I have said, is one way of naming the separation from God, which is "not the way it is supposed to be." But this too is a major way that sin manifests itself: in broken and abusive relationships within the human community.

Psalm 42 testifies eloquently to human longing for God in a time of distress. This longing itself, however, has revealed several aspects of what it means to be human: we are alienated from God, but we also depend on God, and we are intended for relationship with the "God of my life." We are also made for community with others, but rather than living in true community we perpetuate patterns of oppression, pain, and abuse toward one another.

Memory of Past Joy

> These things I remember,
>   as I pour out my soul:
> how I went with the throng,
>   and led them in procession to the house of God,
> with glad shouts and songs of thanksgiving,
>   a multitude keeping festival.
>
> (Ps. 42:4)

The psalm begins with a profound reflection on human longing for God. Yet in the fourth verse, the psalmist moves to remember a time when God did not seem so distant. If we continue to take this as a prayer that shows us something about the human condition, then we have to ask: what does this section suggest about who we are?

To begin with, this verse suggests that we who pray are people not only of present distress (or joy) but people with deep memories of the past. In particular, we remember God's faithfulness in the past and our own particular histories with God. We do not live our lives only aware of the present moment, but with memory of how things used to be.

We all have our own histories that shape our experience of the present time. My own earliest memories of church include the cool of air conditioning in the heat of a Florida summer, the vibrant white of the walls and furniture in the sanctuary that spoke to me of cleanness and calm, the worn red covers of the hymnals out of which we sang and read the Psalms together. The truth is, my default understanding of church can never be divorced from these images of unadorned simplicity and the feel of cool air on my overheated face. So too for the psalmist here: in a time of distress, he returns to a memory of worship leadership in the past, the sounds of his people rejoicing, the joy of keeping festival. This memory informs how he understands what is going on here and now. The psalmist knows what joy felt like, what it sounded like to be in the midst of a singing multitude, and how all of these things spoke of God's faithful presence.

Notice the way the psalmist plays with the language of memory and forgetting in this psalm. Here he says, "These things I remember. . . ." Yet a few verses later he cries out to God, "Why have you forgotten me?" It is as though the writer is saying, "I can remember, God; why can't you?" Memory of God's faithfulness in the past gives the one praying the grounds for calling God to continued faithfulness in the present.

Does this feel presumptuous? Do we have the right to call on God to be with us now, based on God's faithfulness in the past? This can indeed sound impertinent, yet it is an example of prayer that we see over and over in the Psalms and other Scriptures, especially in the Old Testament. Psalm 85, for instance, begins by recounting God's deeds in the past—"LORD, you were favorable to your land, you restored the fortunes of Jacob"—and then proceeds to cry out, "Restore us again, O God of our salvation, and put away your indignation toward us. Will you be angry with us forever?" (vv. 1, 4).[5] "We remember," say the people, "that you have made promises to be with us. You delivered our ancestors in the past. Even when we wandered away, you did not wander away from us. So, since that is the kind of God you are, come and be with us now!"

Christian prayers at the Lord's Supper have long included this kind of remembering of God's faithfulness, leading both to thanksgiving and to a call for God to be present now:

> When we were unfaithful to you
> You kept faith with us,
> Your love remained steadfast.
> When we were slaves in Egypt,
> You broke the bonds of our oppression,
> Brought us through the sea to freedom,
> And made covenant to be our God.
> By a pillar of fire you led us through the desert
> To a land overflowing with milk and honey,
> And set before us the way of life.
> You spoke of love and justice in the prophets,
> And in the Word made flesh you lived among us,
> Manifesting your glory.
> He died that we might live,
> And is risen to raise us to new life.[6]

The beginning of the Great Thanksgiving is a good example of remembering God's faithfulness in the past even if the community may not feel God's nearness in the present.

As this example of eucharistic praying shows us, Christians remember God's past faithfulness particularly through the life, death, and resurrection of Jesus Christ. While the psalmist remembers leading people in procession at a great festival, Christians remember the procession through the streets of Jerusalem on Palm Sunday and the procession to Golgotha just a few days later. We remember the cross, and the tomb, and then the inexplicable appearances of Jesus days later, again alive, on the road and in the upper room. These are our strongest memories of God's faithfulness to us in the past, and these memories can sustain us even in the times when we feel profoundly alone in the present.

Hope

> Why are you cast down, O my soul,
>   and why are you disquieted within me?
> Hope in God, for I shall again praise him,
>   my help and my God.
>
> (Ps. 42:5–6a)

So far the psalm has shown us several important facets of what it means to be human, and especially a human who prays: with the psalmist, we are created to be in communion with God, yet we are painfully separated from living in communion with God and community with others. We are people who know present pain, yet we are also people who remember joy in the past and who sense that the present alienation from God will not last forever. This last dimension of human life—hope for restoration—becomes more clear in verse 5 (verse 11 repeats the lines). It reiterates the hopeful attitude of the one who prays, voicing again the dependence on God for help.

I have suggested that it is helpful to think about Christian prayer as being drawn into the life of the triune God, so that God is simultaneously our source, our goal, and our companion. This does not mean, however, that we leave behind the notion that prayer is *asking*. If God remains the one to whom we pray—asking for help, for guidance, or for love—then built into the practice of prayer already is a hopeful attitude. If we did not have some sense that God could help us in times of trouble, why would we pray at all? The psalm here shows us this aspect of what it means to be a praying human: it means not only to look back at the past, not only to look to the present moment, but also to look to the future with some kind of hope in God who will again help us.

The curious questioning form of Psalm 42 here also depicts an internal tension in the speaker, between the immediate downcast emotional state and the more fundamental reliance on God, which is formed by memory and hope. This tension also shows up in verse 8: "By day the LORD commands his steadfast love, and at night his song is with me, a prayer to the God of my life." Here the speaker reiterates God's command to love him and voices the ongoing prayer that accompanies the person at night, even in the midst of distress. This suggests that we are always already in God's presence, even in distress, whether we realize it or not.

Why are you cast down, O my soul, and why are you disquieted within me? Verses 5 and 11 suggest that those who pray are voicing some hope for the future, some confidence, however remote, that God is (or should be) able to rescue those who are in distress and heal the wounds of creation.

Portrait of Humanity

Psalm 42 does not tell us everything there is to know about what it means to be human. Much more could and should be said by others. Yet this psalm offers a portrait of humanity that is more complex than first appears. From reflection on these few verses, we can glimpse past, present, and future dimensions of human personhood. Present longing reveals a sense that all is not right with the world and yet that we were made to be in communion with God and community with others. Such longing also reveals a hunch that the way things are now is not the way they will remain forever. The middle of the psalm turns to the past, to memory of God's former faithfulness in order to call on God's continued faithfulness in the present. And the refrain "Hope in God, for again I will praise him" shows a profound hope that the praise in the past will return in the future.

The psalm at heart shows the dynamic interplay between our false selves, which live in separation from God (the disquieted soul), and our true selves, which are intended for and restored to communion with God. Though others may say much more about what it means to be human, this basic picture provides a helpful place for us to begin our reflections on prayer.

Questions for Discussion

1. When have you experienced a "thirst for the living God," as described in Psalm 42?
2. What memories of past joy sustain you in the present?
3. How do you maintain hope in God when you know that all is not right with the world?

3

What Then Is Prayer?

"When you are praying, do not heap up empty phrases as the Gentiles do; for they think that they will be heard because of their many words. Do not be like them, for your Father knows what you need before you ask him.
"Pray then in this way:
Our Father in heaven . . ."

—Matthew 6:7–9a

*I*n the first two chapters, I explored prayer by focusing on the two parties involved: God and us. The God to whom we pray, I suggested, stands before us, behind us, and beside us in prayer, so that we not only pray *to* God but also *by the power of* God and even, mysteriously, *beside* God our companion. So prayer invites us to participate in the dynamic life of the triune God. In the second chapter I suggested that we who pray are also dynamic selves, aware that in the present all is not as it should be, yet possessing deep memories of the past and hopes for the future. These reflections already provide some clues about what prayer itself is, but in this chapter we will explore the matter in more depth.

Misunderstandings of Prayer

In order to think about what prayer is, we can learn much from these words of Jesus from the Sermon on the Mount. Notice the first thing that Jesus does: he opens his discussion of prayer by pointing out problematic understandings of prayer. Just before this passage, he advises his listeners not to pray publicly in order to call attention to themselves, but to pray in private. Here he warns against praying with "empty phrases"; again, he seems to be pointing out that too often those who pray are calling attention to themselves rather than calling on God.

We too need to hear these warnings: when we pray, we need to remember that this is an encounter between ourselves and God, not an exercise in public performance. Long-winded prayers are not necessarily a mark of faithfulness. Further, Jesus suggests, prayer is not just a list of our demands to God; as Jesus says, "Your Father knows what you need before you ask him." In prayer we are not supplying information that God does not already have. To be sure, prayer clearly involves asking, for Jesus goes on to outline a prayer with six petitions, including asking for daily bread and forgiveness. (This is a point to which I will return in a later chapter.) When we pray, we rightly raise particular needs before God—for healing, for mercy, for justice, for bread. Yet we do not ask for things as if God did not already anticipate our need. Asking in the context of prayer is a peculiar kind of asking, not to be confused with visiting Santa or entering contract negotiations. (More on this later.)

What other understandings of prayer do we need to question? Though Jesus does not name them, I notice two additional views of prayer in North American culture that deserve caution. One is the notion that prayer is a form of stress reduction or spiritual hygiene. In the mid-twentieth century, theologian Karl Barth addressed a similar concern, saying that prayer is not "an exercise in the cultivation of the soul or spirit, i.e., the attempt to intensify and deepen ourselves, to purify and cleanse ourselves inwardly, to attain clarity and self-control, and finally to set ourselves on a good footing and in agreement with the deity by this preparation."[1] Some of my friends who devote themselves to regular practices of prayer do indeed exude a calm wisdom in the midst of frenzied lives that I find remarkable. They seem to have attained a high degree of "clarity and self-control." When prayer becomes a regular part of living, it does change the way a person relates to the urgent demands of daily routine. Yet if we think of prayer as simply another thing that we do to better our lives, we risk making it about us rather than God. It can become a means to develop our spiritual selves, rather than a practice of turning our

whole selves over to the Holy Mystery. Moreover, we can underesti-
mate the way that prayer might lead, not to comfort, but to profound
discomfort with some aspects of our world today.

I sometimes hear another problematic interpretation of prayer: "All
of life should be prayer." There is something right about this, of
course. If prayer is about living more deeply and intentionally in God,
then surely this is something to strive for all the time. Yet it is too easy
for this statement to become a justification for never pausing for a specific time of prayer. We can then look at our busy schedules and claim
that each task is really prayer. If all of life is prayer, I fear that nothing will really be prayer.

All of these misunderstandings of prayer can be related to one central difficulty at the heart of the praying life: prayer is finally directed
to God, not to ourselves. It is not about calling attention to ourselves
(as "the Gentiles" do in Jesus' teaching); it is about directing attention
to God. It is not about a list of demands; it is about listening for what
God demands of us. It is not about our own best life now; it is about
seeking our true life hidden in the heart of the triune God. And it is not
mistaking our important life activities for the activity of God. Prayer,
indeed, offers an important corrective to this temptation so seductive
to American life. Prayer is not first of all about us, but about God.

The Heart of Prayer: Participation in God

In prayer, then, we need to direct our attention not to ourselves but to
God. Yet prayer does involve us. And this is the mystery. We are intimately involved in the activity of prayer, but paradoxically, it is both
our action and *not* our action!

At the end of the first chapter, I stated, "In prayer, we enter into this
communion, as we acknowledge that God is at once the source of our
prayer, the one to whom we pray, and our companion in prayer. . . .
True prayer is thus participation in God." This is the heart of the matter. When we pray, we not only ask for God to act; we depend on the
fact that God has already acted. Barth again: "God works in us, for we
know not how to pray as we ought. It is the Spirit of God that incites
us and enables us to pray in a fitting manner."[2] So we do indeed pray,
but it is God's Spirit who opens our lips.

And when we pray, we do not do so alone. Go back to Jesus' words
from Matthew: "Pray then in this way: Our Father in heaven. . . ." He
did not say: "*My* Father in heaven." He said "*Our* Father in heaven."
What is the significance of this word?

The key point is this: Jesus is inviting us to pray *with* him when we
pray to the one he called "Father." When we come to prayer in this
way, we realize that—again, even before we open our lips—we already
stand beside the one who is going to draw us into prayer as a part of
his family. We are not alone. On our knees, on our beds, on our feet,
eyes open or closed—each time we enter into prayer in the spirit of
Jesus, we come before God already in relationship to God.

The Spirit empowers our prayer. Jesus Christ accompanies us in
prayer. This already points to the nature of prayer as entry into communion with God. Yet there is one more facet to explore in Jesus'
teaching on prayer. What are we claiming when we call on God as
"Father"?

Much has been written on this topic in recent decades, and for good
reason. When we restrict our language about God to a single mascu-
line image, this easily becomes idolatry. We begin to assume that God
is more like a male than a female, and we project our understandings
of fatherhood onto divinity. People who have known abusive fathers
are likely to be terrified of this God. I and others like me who have
known loving fathers too easily assume that God is just like the won-
derful man who cooked breakfast and made up fantastic stories for us
when we were growing up. Either of these presents problems: those
in the first group shy away from any relationship with God as Father,
while those in the second group reduce the fatherhood of God to
something familiar and safe. For these reasons, we do well to attend
to the whole range of biblical images for God and not restrict our
attention to "Father" alone.

Yet if we abandon Father-language altogether, we miss the marvel
of Jesus' teaching on prayer. If we follow Jesus' lead in calling God
"Father," we may stumble again into this mystery of prayer as participation in God. If God is "Father," then this is a God with whom we
are already in close relationship. This is no far-off deity, observing us
"from a distance." We do not have to convince this God to come and

establish relationship with us; it has already been done. As soon as we utter the word "Father," we acknowledge our dependence on the One who is source of our being and author of our words, who is before us in our creation as well as before us as a listening presence.

And there is more: just as the word "our" points to relationship with Christ, so too does "Father." Christians address God in this way simply because this is the way Jesus spoke and because Jesus invited his followers into his family. When we call on God as "Father," we acknowledge not only the One who made us but also God in Christ who makes a place for us at the family table.

In prayer, then, we enter into communion with the triune God who is before us, within us, and beside us. Patrick of Ireland in the fifth century gave voice to this mystery in his well-known prayer that begins:

> I bind unto myself today
> the strong name of the Trinity,
> by invocation of the same,
> the Three in One, the One in Three.

Later in the prayer, he celebrates the multiple ways in which God surrounds us in prayer:

> Christ be with me, Christ within me,
> Christ behind me, Christ before me,
> Christ beside me, Christ to win me,
> Christ to comfort and restore me,
> Christ beneath me, Christ above me,
> Christ in quiet, Christ in danger,
> Christ in hearts of all that love me,
> Christ in mouth of friend and stranger.[3]

The only odd thing about this otherwise beautiful prayer is that in spite of its Trinitarian opening, it is Christ alone who is described as "with, within, behind, before, and beside" the one praying. The Spirit and the "Father" are less visible. Yet Patrick poetically calls our attention to the God who surrounds us. In prayer we "bind unto ourselves" the strong name of the Trinity, opening our eyes to this mystery all around us.

Prayer as Realization of the True Self

I began by pointing out several misunderstandings of prayer, which I suggested are variations on the central problem of prayer: that we too often direct it toward ourselves rather than God. Yet we are somehow involved in prayer—this is not just an isolated soliloquy within the heart of God! We need to return to the question of the self, which I discussed in the last chapter.

Remember what we learned from Psalm 42: that as humans, we live with painful awareness that things are not as they should be. We struggle with the sense that all is not well with the world; I ventured to identify this with the Christian concept of sin. We know that something is not right. Yet even this awareness suggests that we are made for something more: in Christian terms, we know that we are made to be in communion with God and in community with others. The psalmist additionally lives with memories of God's faithfulness in the past, which give hope for a transformed future.

Prayer gives voice to all of these aspects of our human selves: our pain in the present, our memories of the past, and our hopes for the future. In this way, though prayer is not directed toward ourselves, it is profoundly about ourselves—our *true* selves, fashioned in the image of God and called into communion with that One who is behind, beside, and before us.

Your Father knows what you need before you ask him. What do we need? A deepened relationship with God, to be sure, but this deepened relationship necessarily brings with it a deeper understanding of our true selves: dependent on God who is source of our life, breath of our breath, and living communion. Prayer draws us into this knowledge of God and knowledge of ourselves, which are inextricable. In prayer, we move ever more fully into participation in God—and this participation is nothing other than the realization of our true selves.

Questions for Discussion

1. What misunderstanding of prayer do you think is the most common today?

2. What are the benefits and what are the problems with praying to God as "Father"?
3. Read again the portion of St. Patrick's prayer in this chapter. Where do you most easily recognize Christ's presence? Where do you find it most difficult to notice Christ's presence?

What Does Prayer *Do*?

O my God, I cry by day, but you do not answer;
and by night, but find no rest.

—Psalm 22:2

*W*hen my older daughter was six, she informed me that she did not believe in God. When I asked her why, she responded that she had spoken to God and had not received any answer. Clearly, she reasoned, if there were a God, this God would respond to questioning. No answer, ergo, no God.

Christians of all ages have wrestled with this dilemma for two thousand years. The Psalms themselves witness to the anguish of those who cry out to God and receive no reply. Earlier I developed the portrait of prayer as entrance into the triune life of God. In prayer, we come to participate more fully and consciously in God who is our source, our goal, and our companion in prayer. We bring our memories and hopes, our fears and our joys, and draw them with ourselves into holy communion with the Holy Three-in-One. This sounds lovely, you might say, but it does not address the anguish of those who call out in the night for some kind of real response, only to hear silence. So let's ask the straightforward practical question: what does prayer really do?

As the psalmist attests, prayer does not always (and perhaps does not usually) elicit an immediate clear response from the God to whom we pray. Like my daughter, we often approach God asking for some response, and we hear nothing but silence. What does this mean? Is God not listening? Does God not care? Or—as my daughter suspected—is God not there at all?

Does God Answer Prayer?

The psalmist cries out, "O my God, I cry by day, but you do not answer." The experience of unanswered prayer can be painful, sometimes even life-threatening. Though my daughter's agnosticism in the face of unanswered prayer was relatively minor and temporary, others have known much more wrenching times of unanswered prayers: "O God, save my child." "Take away the cancer." "Protect the lives of your people." In the face of these prayers, it is patently obvious that illness, disaster, and death are not always averted by the prayers of the faithful. We might conclude from this that God does not in fact always answer prayer.

But this is not the only conclusion we might draw. First of all, notice that when we pray, we are already assuming the existence of God, who receives our prayers. So the act of prayer, even the most bitter lament that shakes a fist at God, still retains some shred of faith that there is a God who needs to hear our rage. Whatever prayer does, it presumes the existence of God with whom we already have some relationship.

Second, we have already said that when we pray, we are not giving God new information. As Jesus taught, "Your Father knows what you need before you ask him." Prayer does not initiate the relationship between us and God; it enacts the relationship that God has already established. Prayer does not simply consist of call and response, in which we cry out and God provides an immediate and obvious answer. Yet we do not want to go to the extreme of saying that God does not respond to our prayers at all, because Jesus teaches his disciples to pray, even saying, "Whatever you ask for in prayer, believe that you have received it, and it will be yours" (Mark 11:24). Prayer is not a straightforward list of demands to be met or negotiated, but it does involve laying our needs before God in faith that we will be heard. How do we solve this dilemma?

Part of the solution comes from a reconsideration of what prayer is. Go back to the portrait of prayer we have been developing since the first chapter: prayer is participation in the triune life of God. If this is so, then prayer is not simply our address to a God who stands somehow apart from us waiting for our petitions. We often have the mistaken impression that we cannot act simultaneously with God. We think we have separate, independent agency. But as we have already reflected, God is not only the one who receives our prayers but is the one who prompts our praying and accompanies us in praying. Even before we receive some kind of answer, God is already at work in and through our prayers.

We can see this in two different ways: in the work of the Spirit and in the intercession of Christ. First, when we pray, the Holy Spirit is already acting through us. As C. S. Lewis put it, "If the Holy Spirit speaks in the [one praying], then in prayer God speaks to God. . . . 'God did (or said) it' and 'I did (or said) it' can both be true."[1] So God does not only listen to us pray, but God is already at work praying in and through us by the power of the Spirit.

Second, when we pray we do not pray alone, but with and through Jesus Christ. In his reflections on the Heidelberg Catechism (one of the most important Reformed Protestant confessions of the sixteenth century), Karl Barth focused attention on the last question and answer of that document:

Q. 129. What is the meaning of the little word "Amen"?

A. Amen means: this shall truly and certainly be. For my prayer is much more certainly heard by God than I am persuaded in my heart that I desire such things from him.[2]

From the confidence of Heidelberg's answer, Barth concludes that prayer influences God's action, even God's very existence. When we pray, we are praying in and through Jesus Christ, and God cannot help but listen to Jesus. When God looks at all of humanity, God sees Jesus Christ. We are therefore already in the presence of God, and when we pray, we are repeating what was already prayed by Jesus.[3]

To see an example of this, go back to the words of Psalm 22 at the opening of this chapter: "O my God, I cry by day, but you do not answer; and by night, but find no rest." These are the words of the lamenting psalmist, to be sure, but they are more than that. They are also the words that directly follow Jesus' cry from the cross: "My God, my God, why have you forsaken me?" In the crucifixion, Jesus cried out these opening words of Psalm 22, and many scholars think that when he cried out in this way, he was anticipating the rest of the psalm. If this is right, then we can hear the words "I cry by day, but you do not answer" paradoxically, as both the cry of separation from God and the cry of God's own heart. When we pray, even when no answer seems to come, it may be that the cry itself is a participation in the lament of Christ.

How Does God Answer Prayer?

In part, then, we can see that the dilemma of "what prayer does" can be addressed by rethinking the relationship between "our" praying and "God's" answering. The act of prayer is more complex than simply laying petitions at the divine throne. Prayer itself is simultaneously an act of God and our own act, our own expression of need. This suggests that sometimes God's response emerges in the act of praying itself.

Yet we can say more. As Scripture and Christian tradition attest, people receive answers to prayer beyond the act of prayer itself. Furthermore, what appear to be "unanswered prayers" may not in fact be unanswered at all. It may be that God responds to our prayers, but not in the way we expect. Specifically, answer to prayer may come

- as judgment on our petitions;
- as redeemed hope on the far side of suffering; or
- as encounter with Christ in the midst of suffering.

An example of the first comes from a recent book on the Civil War. According to historian Mark Noll, Abraham Lincoln reflected about the two sides of that war: "'Both sides read the same Bible and pray to the same God.' And since they prayed for different outcomes, 'the prayers of both could not be answered.'"[4] As much as I appreciate Lincoln's stark observation, I think there is more to be said here. It may be that God did indeed answer both sets of prayers—but answering does not always mean saying yes. Sometimes God's answer comes as judgment, as a profound no if our requests serve to perpetuate injustice and oppression.

At other times, God answers prayer not by preventing suffering but by offering hope and life on the far side of suffering. For instance, Hebrews 5:7 says that "Jesus offered up prayers and supplications, with loud cries and tears, to the one who was able to save him from death, and he was heard because of his reverent submission." But there is a problem here. Although God "was able to save him from death," Jesus was not prevented from dying. Indeed, he met death in a particularly painful and horrific way, even though this verse implies that God could have saved him. What could it mean to say that Jesus' prayers were heard, even though it is obvious that he was not spared death? This can be answered (at least in part) by setting Jesus' prayers in the larger context of not only his crucifixion but also his resurrection. To begin with, the portrayal of Jesus' cries and tears in prayer emphasizes Jesus' deep solidarity with humanity, because his prayers do not simply deliver him from sufferings.[5] In this way, his experience resembles those of many others who pray and yet are not prevented from pain and even death. Furthermore, though God did not save Jesus from experiencing real human death, this was not the end of the story. God then raised Jesus from death, "saving him from death" in a more profound sense. In this way, God did answer Jesus' prayers, offering life not only to him, but to "all who obey him" (Heb. 5:9). Sometimes the answer to prayers comes in utterly new and unexpected ways, not sparing us pain, but redeeming us from it.

Yet again, God may answer prayer not by preventing suffering but by accompanying us in the midst of it. In the 2007 book *Mother Teresa: Come Be My Light*, author Brian Kolodiejchuk shows a side of Mother Teresa previously unknown to most people: her complete lack of a sense of God's presence during nearly fifty years of her life. For decades, she experienced this absence as deep spiritual pain, leading her even to doubt the existence of God. For decades, she lived with a profound sense of unanswered prayer. Yet eventually, with the help of her confessor Joseph Neuner, Mother Teresa came to understand this pain itself in a new way: not as the utter absence of God, but as identification with the suffering of Christ on the cross. As one reporter has written, "For all that she had expected and even craved to share in Christ's passion, she had not anticipated that she might recapitulate the particular moment on the cross when he asks, 'My God, my God, why have you forsaken me?' . . . Neuner would later write, 'It was the redeeming experience of her life when she realized that the night of her heart was the special share she had in Jesus' passion.'"[6] In this remarkable case, we can see the answer to prayer coming not in the prevention of suffering, but in the recognition that the suffering itself is a participation in Christ.

How does God answer prayer? Certainly some people tell stories of God responding to their prayers in clear and direct ways: through guidance in a time of discernment, through love in a time of loneliness, through comfort in a time of grief. Yet we need to recognize that God also answers prayers in the less obvious, and more difficult, ways suggested above. Sometimes, as in the case of the South in the Civil War, God responds to prayers by saying no. Sometimes, as in Jesus' own words from the cross, God responds by saying, "Yes, but not in the way you think." And sometimes, as in the life of Mother Teresa, God answers prayer by pointing out how the experience of spiritual darkness itself may in fact be a revelation of the God-forsakenness of Christ on the cross.

Does Prayer Work if We Do Not Feel It?

One tricky question remains: does prayer work when we do not genuinely feel it? This brings us back to a popular view of prayer we examined in chapter 3: prayer as spiritual hygiene, as good exercise for our own well-being. If prayer is supposed to enhance our sense of calm and poise in the midst of a chaotic world, then what happens when we do not experience it as nourishment or calm? Is prayer really prayer if we do not feel prayerful?

As we saw in the previous chapter, the danger in this question is that it focuses attention on us rather than on God. To be sure, when prayer becomes a regular part of living, it does change the way a person interacts with the world, leading at times to a deep sense of calm. Yet if we think of prayer as simply a means to the end of our greater well-being, we risk making it about us rather than God.

One contemporary Orthodox Christian writer, reflecting on prayer, has said, "We are to seek, not 'experiences,' but only Jesus Christ."[7] If prayer is about directing attention to God rather than ourselves, then the adequacy of prayer does not depend on the intensity of our own experience. Again, Mother Teresa offers a clear example of this insight: she described nearly fifty years of spiritual dryness, during which she had no profound feeling of God's nearness. Yet she continued the hard work of daily prayer, coming eventually to the realization that the feeling of absence itself was a bitter experience of Christ's passion—not a separation from God at all, but deep knowledge of the agony of God in the crucifixion.

Theologian Karl Rahner also helpfully reminds us that prayer is not to be judged by what kind of experience it evokes. Instead, prayer depends on forgetting the self, on not being preoccupied with our own experience of prayer. Like human love, prayer is only real when we do not inspect it. Rahner observes that in this respect, both love and prayer are like a rifle, which we cannot take apart for inspection and shoot at the same time. "One can only know whether the noble act of the heart really succeeds when one does it and forgets what one is doing."[8]

Prayer, then, is one instance of the paradox of the gospel: that in order to find our lives, we must lose them. Once we give up our preoccupation with ourselves and our experiences of prayer, we might realize that through prayer, our very selves are being reshaped—not by our own efforts, but by the unpredictable mercy of God.

What does prayer do? The act of prayer turns our attention to God, giving voice to our dependence and our need. But answers to prayers come often in disguise, not as obvious rewards for our efforts. If we understand prayer as participation in the triune God, then we can see that the "answer" to prayer may be the awareness of the Spirit empowering our words, the judgment of God on our false or misguided words, or even the encounter with the suffering Christ in the midst of our pain.

Questions for Discussion

1. Describe a time when you experienced God's answer to a prayer. What was it like?
2. Describe a time when you did not receive an obvious answer to prayer. What was that like?
3. Can you identify times in your life when God may have answered prayers with judgment, with hope on the far side of suffering, or with awareness of Christ's presence in the midst of suffering?

5

What Makes Prayer Christian?

Lord Jesus Christ, Son of God, have mercy on me, a sinner.
—The Jesus Prayer

When I was studying in India after college, I encountered many sorts of prayers that were different from those of my own Protestant Christian upbringing. In Varanasi, a friend and I took an early morning boat ride on the quiet Ganges River, watching the sun rise over the burning *ghats*, where the bodies of the dead were being gradually consumed by flame. We heard the chanted prayers of the priests by the fires and the distant voices of other priests at prayer in temples lining the sacred river. Near the end of our ride, the boat guide presented us with tiny boats made of leaves, in which were votive candles. He lit the candles for us and instructed us to place the boats in the river, where they could float down to the sea. These too were prayers, fragile floating intercessions, set aflame and sent off to an unknown horizon. Prayers by the funeral pyres, prayers in the temples, prayers floating down the river.

To my own encounters with prayer in Varanasi, you might add your own experience or knowledge of Jewish blessings, Muslim daily prayers, Tibetan Buddhist prayer wheels. Is there anything that all of these practices share? What characterizes Christian prayer as distinctive?

Christian Praying amid a World of Religious Praying

It is good to acknowledge what Christian prayers have in common with the prayers of other religious traditions. Of course, not all religious traditions include prayers. Yet many traditions do include disciplined practices in which people focus attention beyond the daily tasks of living to a deeper, more profound dimension of reality. Christians are not the only people in the world who regularly sit, kneel, or prostrate themselves before God. We are not the only ones who light candles, whisper or chant, or shout praise and petitions to a power greater than ourselves. The impulse to pray is not unique to Christians.

But we can say even more than this. Not only should we recognize what we hold in common with followers of other religious paths. Christians can also learn some things about prayer from our sisters and brothers of other religions. For instance, the Roman Catholic spiritual writer and Trappist monk Thomas Merton spent the last decade of his life learning much from Buddhist practices. In his "Asian Journal," written during extensive travels shortly before his death, he wrote, "I think we have now reached a stage of (long overdue) religious maturity at which it may be possible for someone to remain perfectly faithful to a Christian and Western monastic commitment, and yet to learn in depth from, say, a Buddhist or Hindu discipline and experience. I believe that some of us need to do this in order to improve the quality of our own monastic life."[1] Like Merton, we too might learn from prayer practices of other religious traditions that aid in focusing our attention, stilling the restlessness of the body, or quieting the chatter of the mind. Christians need not be afraid of learning wisdom from people who have developed patterns of contemplation and prayer apart from faith in Jesus Christ.

Christian Prayer: In the Name of Jesus

Yet Christian prayer is not just like any other kind of praying. It is distinctive, because Christians alone pray "in the name of Jesus." If we have to identify what it is that distinguishes Christian prayer from other prayers, it is this: that we offer prayers in and through Jesus' name.

What does this mean? Is praying in the name of Jesus simply a matter of adding the words "we ask this in the name of Jesus Christ" before declaring "Amen" at the end of each prayer? It is easy for this phrase to become thoughtless repetition, a kind of sign-off at the end of prayer, like "yours truly" or "sincerely." But Christian pastors and writers through the centuries have suggested that there is deeper significance to praying "in Jesus' name" that helps us to discern the heart of truly Christian prayer.

One Eastern Orthodox monk, reflecting on the phrase "in the name of Jesus," points out that the English words here do not do justice to the diversity of Greek expressions in the New Testament. He points out that what we read as "in the name" actually reflects three different phrases that are better understood as "on the name," "toward the name," and "in the name":

> In *epi to onomati*, one leans "on" the name; it is the foundation on which one builds. . . . In *eis to onoma*, there is a movement "toward" the name, a dynamic relationship of finality which sees the name as the goal to be attained. . . . In *en to onomati*, the attitude is static; it expresses the repose which follows the attainment of the goal. . . . Our spirit is transported "into" the name, within the name, it is united to the name and makes its abode there.[2]

In this view, offering prayer "in the name of Jesus" draws us into a more complex relationship with Jesus Christ than we first thought. The name of Jesus is not just a required tagline but is the foundation, goal, and resting place in which we offer our prayers.

Lord Jesus Christ, Son of God, have mercy on me, a sinner. This little petition, called the "Jesus Prayer," is popular in many Eastern Orthodox traditions. It offers one example of praying "in the name of Jesus," since it attributes particular significance to praying the name of Jesus itself. Christians through the centuries who have prayed in this way usually repeat the prayer so that it accompanies their breathing, inhaling as they recite (aloud or internally), "Lord Jesus Christ, Son of God," and exhaling on the petition "have mercy on me, a sinner." This repetition over time becomes a natural accompaniment to breathing, so that the one praying constantly turns her attention to Jesus Christ, the source of mercy. The Orthodox monk whom we have already heard reflecting on "the name of Jesus" emphasizes that the Jesus Prayer is "not a technique but an act of love. It expresses a direct relationship between persons."[3] One cannot really pray the name of Jesus without a living relationship with Jesus. Repeating the name, then, actually draws the one praying to participate in the name of

Jesus, which is his power and life. Though it might appear that such a practice is no more than empty words, Orthodox practitioners of this prayer underscore its vital connection to Jesus' own life. "We do not remain exterior to the name invoked, but the invocation allows us to 'participate in the holy name of Jesus.'"[4]

The Jesus Prayer gives one example of Christian praying that is at once calling on the name of Jesus, striving to live toward the name of Jesus, and abiding in the name of Jesus. But what about the rest of Christian praying? What are we to say about prayer in Jesus' name apart from the specific Jesus Prayer?

New Testament scholar Oscar Cullmann focuses particularly on the way the Gospel of John uses the phrase "in the name of Jesus," since in that Gospel, Jesus repeatedly tells his disciples to pray (or ask) in his name (see John 14:13, 14; 15:16; and 16:23–26). Cullmann emphasizes that with these words, Jesus is promising his disciples that he will continue to be with them, even though he is going to his death. So prayer "in Jesus' name" points to the real living presence of Christ with his community. During his lifetime, the disciples ask Jesus to teach them to pray (as in Luke 11), but as he prepares to depart, the disciples need something more: a promise that they will not be left as orphans. He does promise that the Spirit will be sent as Comforter and Advocate. "But first of all the formula 'pray in the name of Jesus' means that in their prayer the disciples largely continue to need the presence of Jesus as during his earthly life, and that this help will be given them because he will not be absent."[5] Prayer in the name of Jesus calls on the risen Jesus as our present companion in prayer.

In addition, prayer in the name of Jesus calls on Jesus as intercessor before God the Father. "This intercession of the one who has been exalted to God . . . means that we need his help to pray, and that on the basis of the presence of the Son with the Father we for our part are directly joined with the Father in our prayer."[6] As John's Gospel makes clear, after his resurrection Jesus is simultaneously present with his disciples and present with God, whom he calls "Father." This means that when disciples pray in his name, they not only affirm Jesus at their side but through Jesus stand in the presence of "the Father."

In the Reformed Protestant tradition, prayer "in Jesus' name" is often linked with Jesus' role as intercessor. The Westminster Larger

Catechism, composed in 1647 as a teaching tool and aid to preaching, says this:

> To pray in the name of Christ is, in obedience to his command, and in confidence on his promises, to ask mercy for his sake: not by bare mentioning of his name; but by drawing our encouragement to pray, and our boldness, strength, and hope of acceptance in prayer, from Christ and his mediation.[7]

The Westminster Catechism goes on to emphasize that we ourselves have no access to God without a mediator, and Christ is the only mediator. This underscores what Cullmann has pointed out: that when we pray in the name of Jesus, we stand in the presence of Jesus who is joined with us and also joined with the "Father." He thus mediates between humanity and God, representing God to us and representing us to God in prayer.

Christian Prayer: Participation in the Trinity

What does it mean to pray in the name of Jesus? As we have heard from the Jesus Prayer and from Cullmann, language that names Jesus Christ is a part of such praying, but praying in Jesus' name goes far beyond mere recital of those words. Praying in Jesus' name means two basic things: (1) to pray in a way that is consistent with Jesus' character, and (2) to pray out of our unity with Jesus, joining our voices with his.

First, as Cullmann reminds us, to do something "in the name" of someone is to act on that person's behalf, in a way that is in keeping with her actions. For instance, if I sign a document in the name of my husband, I stand in his place, and thus I sign only if I am certain that he would do so himself. So also with praying: to pray in Jesus' name is to offer words and petitions that are consistent with what we know of Jesus. Concretely, this suggests that no matter what words we say at the conclusion of a prayer, if we pray for the utter annihilation of our enemies, this is simply not "in Jesus' name." Specifically Christian prayer always reflects the character of the one who called us to love our enemies and to pray for those who persecute us.

Second, to pray "in Jesus' name" returns us to a theme we echoed earlier: in Christian praying, we are offering prayers in the voice of

Jesus, our companion and intercessor. If we really offer prayers in the name of Jesus Christ, we are no longer speaking simply for ourselves; we speak as those joined with the crucified and risen One. We offer prayers with Christ, who is himself united with his Father. Karl Barth, the Swiss Reformed theologian, emphasizes this by saying that when Christians pray to God in the name of Christ, "their asking is enclosed in his asking, their petition is a 'repetition of his petition.'"[8] Christ is the great pray-er; our prayers are expressions of our unity with his praying.

Praying in Jesus' name, then, is participation in Jesus Christ, and through him, participation in the life of the triune God. Once again, we are back at the heart of the Trinity. Praying in Christ is participating in the dynamic relationship between Son and Father (as John puts it) and in the Spirit that binds them together.

Christian Prayer and Other Kinds of Praying

What then are we to say about the prayers of Hindu holy men on the banks of the Ganges? What are we to say about our Muslim sisters and brothers who offer prayers five times daily facing Mecca? Does God receive these prayers and the prayers of other people who reach out to something they call "God" but not in the name of Jesus?

An adequate answer to this question requires extended conversation with particular people in non-Christian communities. This is not a question we can answer simply or alone. Yet on the basis of our discussion so far, we can say at least two things:

- We do not determine whose prayers God hears. God is free to listen, to inspire, to move as God wills.
- We pray on the basis of what we know about God, which is revealed in Jesus Christ. Christian prayer therefore is prayer in Jesus' name.

First, the mystery of God is far greater than we can know, and so we need to exercise humility in judging whom God hears in prayer. Our triune God is free to do far more than we ask or imagine. Therefore, in this increasingly religiously plural world, we need not fear those who pray differently than we do. Indeed, we might approach conversation with other religious communities with joyful curiosity, asking how they pray and expecting that God might already be at work there before we arrive.

Second, we pray according to what we know of God in Christ and by the power of the Spirit. This is why we pray "in Jesus' name." Christian prayer draws us into deeper relationship with Jesus, and through Jesus, into the triune life of God. Yet prayer in Jesus' name is not just about uttering formulaic language; it is about following the way of Jesus. Could it be that some people who have never heard the name of Jesus still pray "in Jesus' name" because they live in a way that is consistent with Jesus' pattern of self-giving love? Conversely, could it be that some people pray using the correct language and yet do not pray "in Jesus' name" because they fail to embody the life to which he calls us?

Christian prayer may resemble some other sorts of praying, and Christians can learn from the prayer practices of other religious traditions. Yet Christians alone pray in and through the name of Jesus. We need not regard this as an exclusive act, but a way of praying that draws on the most reliable source of knowledge we have about the God to whom we pray. We pray in and through Jesus' "name," which means we pray in keeping with Jesus' character and Jesus' activity with the world as crucified and risen Savior. As we pray, so shall we seek to live: loving God and loving all those neighbors whom God places in our path.

Questions for Discussion

1. What opportunities have you had to witness the prayers of religious communities who are not Christian? What have you learned from these experiences?
2. How have you understood praying "in Jesus' name"?
3. Do you think Christians should pray in Jesus' name in the presence of people who are not Christians? Why or why not?

6

Times of Prayer

Satisfy us with your love in the morning,
*   and we will live this day in joy and praise.*
        — Based on Psalm 90:14, *Book of Common Worship*

Stay with us, Lord, for it is evening, and the day is almost over.
                                —Luke 24:29, adapted

*W*hen I was in seminary, I became acquainted with Holy Cross Abbey, a Trappist monastery in Berryville, Virginia, set amid rolling hills and cow pastures in the beautiful Shenandoah Valley. During those years, I spent a few weekends on retreat in the guesthouse there, swathed in silence and solitude that was punctuated only by meals with the other guests and visits to the chapel to pray with the monks. Crunching along the gravel road from the guesthouse to the chapel in the dawning light, I could already hear the bells calling us to morning prayer. As I slipped into the back of the still-dark chapel, the chanting began from the choir: "O Lord, open my lips, and my mouth will proclaim your praise." The prayers continued later with the petition "Satisfy us with your love in the morning, and we will live this day in joy and praise." The day thus began by evoking God's abundant love and calling us to live out of that love for the rest of our waking hours.

Years later, on retreat at Mepkin Abbey in the low country of South Carolina, I found myself trudging along another dusty road under the low branches of live oak trees, making my way from the guesthouse to the chapel for evening prayer at dusk. This time invited to sit in the choir, I was handed the community's book of Psalms from which they pray and welcomed into the chanting of the hours, the specific times when the community prayed together. "Stay with us, Lord, for it is evening, and the day is almost over," we summoned Christ, as the sun sank behind the Spanish moss.

Morning and evening, communities like these pause to offer prayers together. Monastic communities have long been committed to regular times of prayer, designating eight specific hours in the day as occasions to stop from their labor and pray. St. Benedict of Nursia, the sixth-century leader who established the rule still followed by many religious orders today, based this schedule on his reading of Psalm 119:

> The prophet says: "Seven times daily I have sung your praises" (Ps. 119:164). We will cleave to this sacred number if we perform our monastic duties at Lauds, Prime, Tierce, Sext, None, Vespers and Compline. The same prophet says of the Night Office: "I arose at midnight to confess to You" (Ps. 119:62). In the Day Office, therefore, we ought to praise our Creator for His just judgments, and at night we will rise to confess to Him.[1]

Monasteries that follow the Benedictine rule still gather for prayer at these hours: at the beginning of the day (which usually combines Lauds and Prime), midmorning (Tierce), noon (Sext), midafternoon (None), evening (Vespers), and just before bed (Compline), as well as the middle of the night (Vigils). Their days are defined by times of communal prayer.

Yet most of us do not live in monastic communities that are set up for such regular hours of prayer. Most Christians live their lives in the world of jobs and family routines, pulled by the demands of the school bell, the soccer practice, the business meeting, and the need to get dinner on the table in a timely fashion. For us, the very real question is "When are we supposed to pray? When do we find time to pray in the midst of all the other competing demands of our lives?"

Pray without Ceasing?

Earlier chapters have addressed big questions of prayer: Who is the God to whom we pray? Who are we who pray? What is prayer and what does it really do? What is Christian prayer in the midst of a world of other prayers? With this chapter, we move into a series of more practical discussions around the question "*How* do we pray?" In this chapter we will focus on the issue of *when* we pray.

In his first letter to the church in Thessalonica, Paul simply said, "Pray without ceasing" (1 Thess. 5:17). Pray all the time? How is such a thing possible? Perhaps we might dismiss Paul as hopelessly naive, living as he did at a time when the Christian community still expected Jesus to return at any moment and bring in the kingdom of God in its fullness. Of course they could pray all the time, if they thought the world as we know it was about to end!

Pray without ceasing. Though noble in its intention, this exhortation can lead to two problems: first, it can lead to the misunderstanding that we are to be on our knees in the choir or in our closets twenty four hours a day, letting the laundry pile up and our children fend for themselves on doughnuts and instant oatmeal. Yet I do not think even Paul meant this; he himself traveled, spoke to people in private and in public, and engaged in activities we might not automatically call "prayer." So whatever he meant in calling for constant prayer, he was clearly not calling for complete separation from the world of commerce and political interaction.

On the other hand, this call to "pray without ceasing" might play into a misunderstanding of prayer that we encountered in chapter 3: the problem with claiming that "all of life is prayer." As we saw, it is too easy for this statement to become a justification for never pausing for a specific time of prayer. We can then look at our busy schedules and claim that each task is really prayer. If all of life is prayer, I fear that nothing will really be prayer.

These are real concerns of which we need to beware: interpreting prayer as withdrawal from the world and abandonment of our daily tasks, or interpreting all of our daily tasks themselves as prayer. Either of these views is inadequate to answer the question "When do we pray?"

St. Benedict, in setting up his rule for monastic living, exhorted the monks to "pray without ceasing," but he did not mean by this either a complete withdrawal from the tasks of daily living or a complete dissolving of prayer into the everyday tasks of cooking and cleaning. Rather, he set up a schedule for his monks to turn to prayer at regular times of day so that the rest of their work might be in a spirit of prayer.

This is the promise of Paul's command: not to ignore the daily tasks by turning to God in prayer, but periodically to interrupt our daily tasks with moments of prayer so that everything else is shaped by that attitude. "Pray without ceasing" then means learning to turn to God in prayer in the midst of all our daily tasks—all throughout the day—so that "all of life" comes to be prayer.

Making Appointments

But this does take discipline. In order to learn to pray, we have to set aside regular times to wrench our attention away from the urgent items on our agenda and listen for the movement of God's Spirit within us, which might remind us of what is truly urgent. As one wise friend reminds me, "If we don't 'make' time to pray, we won't 'take' time to pray."

Another friend of mine wisely sets real appointments with God, writing them on her calendar and protecting those times to make sure that she does not let other things creep into her commitment to pray. Yet another friend, a pastor busy during the Easter season, programmed his PDA to set off the alarm and remind him "Christ is risen!" every afternoon at 3:00 for the seven weeks of Easter. This message prompted him to stop whatever he was doing and offer a moment of praise and thanks for God's saving work in the world.

Karl Rahner, a Roman Catholic theologian, agrees with these friends and with Benedict that we need to pray at regular times. But everyday prayer too easily becomes routine, without true attention to the triune God. Rahner acknowledges that "the everyday routinizes prayer in the everyday."[2] We may indeed make prayer into an empty act, or we may avoid prayer because it does not feel authentic. Yet "everyday prayer is the prerequisite and consequence of the great and noble hours of prayer."[3] That is, even if it seems empty and our attention wanders, regular times of prayer accustom us to paying attention to God in other moments of life.

I struggle continually with keeping the discipline of daily prayer. For me, it works best when I make appointments not only with God but with other people to help me pray. In the past several years, off and on, I have followed the pattern of morning and evening prayer as developed in the ecumenically informed *Book of Common Worship* (BCW) of the Presbyterian Church (USA). With the monks at Holy Cross and Mepkin Abbeys, and with Christians in many other places around the world, I begin morning prayers of thanksgiving and intercession with the words "Satisfy us with your love in the morning, and we will live this day in joy and praise." The rising of the sun is a natural time to pause and give thanks, listen for God, and try to look with God at the day before me. Yet I keep this pattern more faithfully when I meet with another friend or small group to pray together. In one place where I worked, a colleague and I pledged to meet in his office each morning at 8:30 when we were both there, to read Scripture and offer prayer together. For a couple of years at the school where I now teach, I met with another good friend once or twice a week to follow the same pattern from the BCW. Setting aside time and having someone else hold me accountable has made me more consistent in prayer.

This practice may not be practical for everyone, and there are other ways to prompt regular occasions for prayer in the day. For instance, some people find it useful to keep a prayer list of people and situations for which to pray. You might keep this list at your desk or on the kitchen counter—or even in your calendar—so that it reminds you to pray when you see it during the day. One of my colleagues keeps such a list at home, in a space where he prays each morning, and in this way he remembers all of his students each day before coming into the classroom to teach. If you keep this kind of prayer list handy, it also makes it easy to add names or situations for which you want to give thanks or ask for help as you move through each day. In this way, a list can be both a prompting device to pray regularly and a way to prepare for the next time you pray.

Mealtime prayers are also appointments I make with my family and God, when we give thanks for our food and for the world, usually in the form of a sung blessing. Are we always devoutly attending to the movement of God among and around us during these prayers? Hardly. As often as not, my children simply want to get through it so that they can eat, and I am desperately trying to keep them from kicking each other under the table as we sing, "God, bless to us our bread." Yet moments erupt from time to time that demonstrate the value of this discipline. They reach their hands out to us before they plunge into their food. They wait for the community to gather (even if with complaints and rumbling stomachs) before attending to their own immediate hunger. They learn the language of thanksgiving associated with eating so that such gratitude might surface at other moments even away from the family table.

When Do We Pray?

Morning and evening, mealtime and bedtime are common times that people make appointments to pray. But you may find other times work best, like 3:00 in the afternoon in the midst of a busy season to stop and remember that Christ is risen. More important than the exact time is the regular habit of setting aside time for focused attention on the God who is source, companion, and goal of our lives. Establishing a habit of meeting God in prayer may then shape a life of continuous prayer.

Again, Karl Rahner is helpful: Each time we stop for prayer will not be deeply meaningful. Not every voiced prayer will emerge from the depth of our heart. "Sometimes [everyday prayer] may appear to come just from the lips and not from the heart. But isn't it better that at least the lips are blessing God than when the entire human being becomes mute?"[4] As every singer knows, developing a voice takes practice. So also with praying: setting aside the time, even when it feels like a chore, even when our heart is not in it, is practice. Over time, regular patterns of prayer attune us to the movement of God in the off-hours, so that indeed we might move toward Paul's vision of prayer without ceasing.

Surely prayers will emerge not only when we make time on the calendar, but when we least expect it: in the car, in the classroom, on a walk with the family. But we are more accustomed to pray spontaneously when we develop some practice of disciplined prayer. If we begin to build habits of thanking God and turning to God for help through patterns of prayer, we are more attuned to saying "Thank you" and "Lord, have mercy" all the time. We might say that the disciplined time is the "backbone" and structure for prayer, while the spontaneous prayers are the natural exercises of our "muscles" that have been developed over time. These times of prayer emerge unexpectedly and without prescription. They are our more immediate responses to the work of God we encounter in the midst of life.[5]

As I said in earlier chapters, prayer is participation in the life of the triune God. It is attending to the movement of the Spirit that leads us at odd moments to say, "Thank you," or "Have mercy." It is attending to Jesus Christ our companion who prays with and for us. It is directing our attention to God our faithful parent, who creates all people, loves us despite our waywardness, and sends Jesus to display that love for the world. If this is what we mean by prayer, then these are surely attentive attitudes that we can exercise at all times. Yet how do we learn such a posture of prayer? Through regular practice. Seven or eight times a day is not a magic number to cultivate such attentiveness, but the wisdom of Benedict is that we need practice praying at certain times in order to learn how to pray at all times.

Questions for Discussion

1. When do you make time to pray?
2. Do you agree that setting regular appointments to pray encourages us to "pray without ceasing"? Why or why not?
3. What other strategies help you to make regular time for prayer?

Contexts of Prayer

Whenever you pray, go into your room and shut the door and pray to your Father who is in secret; and your Father who sees in secret will reward you.

—Matthew 6:6

*I*n the last chapter, we focused on the question "When do we pray?" In that discussion, I suggested that Christians have found many ways of answering the "When?" question, but the key point is to develop some kind of regular schedule of prayer. Whether it is morning and evening, or the monastic hours, or the mid afternoon electronic reminder that "Christ is risen," we learn to pray all the time by praying at specific times. But this raises a related question: *Where* do we pray? When we devote our attention to God in prayer, should that be public or private? Alone or with others?

Praying "in Secret"

Whenever you pray, go into your room and shut the door. In this passage from Matthew's Gospel, Jesus teaches the importance of private "secret" prayer in contrast to the prayer offered by "the hypocrites," who pray in public in order to be seen by others. Is Jesus saying that we should never pray with other people? That all corporate prayer is wrong? I do not think this is what Jesus means; clearly, as an observant Jew, he himself prayed with others in temple and synagogue and would have prayed at mealtimes with his family and friends. But he is countering one of the misunderstandings of prayer we examined in chapter 3: when we pray, we need to remember that this is an encounter between ourselves and God, not an exercise in public performance. For this reason, personal prayer "in secret" is a vital component of a life of prayer.

Lutheran pastor and professor Lisa Dahill suggests that though public worship is at the heart of the Christian tradition, most Christians need help really engaging the mystery we celebrate in worship. This deep engagement will not happen if we only pray once a week on Sunday mornings. Dahill provides a series of contemplative prayer practices rooted in the movements of Christian worship that "are intended to help you learn over time both to worship more fully and to let worship encompass ever more of your 'normal' life at home, at church, and in the world."[1]

One of her discussions focuses on prayers of confession. Corporate prayers of confession, vital to many Christian worshiping communities, provide an opportunity to acknowledge our sin before God and receive the word of forgiveness that has come in Jesus Christ. But, as Dahill points out, "the safe, anonymous practice of general confession in worship, using prayers pre-printed in bulletin or worship book, is inadequate as the sole vehicle for this process" of confession. General confession alone allows us to avoid real confrontation with the specificity of sin in our lives, which allows us to avoid real repentance. "The fact that we know we are sinners does not mean we know our sin," says Dahill. "Sin's real-life constellations and configurations are as particular as each one of us before God."[2] To help with this, she suggests engaging in individual prayers of examen (examination of conscience) that focus attention on individual thanksgiving and confession at the end of each day or week. This practice can then deepen one's engagement in prayers of confession in corporate worship.

Such prayer "in secret" allows us to attend to God in a way that is, paradoxically, both more and less self-conscious. At its best, as Dahill suggests regarding prayers of confession, individual prayer can turn our attention to God's work in the specificity of our lives. We can offer thanks for particular gifts; we can acknowledge and repent of specific sinful actions; we can offer up petitions for people and situations by name. We can sit silently and listen for God speaking directly into our lives. In these ways, personal prayers are *more* self-conscious, more attentive to our particular selves in relation to the triune God.

On the other hand, prayer "in secret" is also *less* self-conscious than public prayer. Without others around us whose opinions we value, we can worry less about how our words sound or whether we have the theological principles exactly right as we engage in prayer. We may still worry about saying the wrong thing to God, but when we pray alone, at least we do not worry about saying the wrong thing in front of other people. Jesus' words in Matthew are thus good news both for those who are articulate pray-ers, for whom public prayer becomes a display of theological prowess, and for those who are timid pray-ers, for whom public prayer can be excruciating. For both groups, prayer "in secret" returns attention where it belongs: to prayer as encounter between the true self and the triune God.

Praying in Families and Close Communities

In the sixteenth and seventeenth centuries, many church reformers focused new attention on families as vitally important places for regular prayer. In the Reformed Protestant tradition, families were encouraged to pray morning and evening, as well as before and after meals, and "heads of households" had particular responsibility to nurture these patterns. These efforts at family worship were intended to deepen the piety of ordinary Christians, as a supplement to Sunday worship services. Though recent studies suggest that the efforts to establish regular family worship habits were "neither universal nor consistent," there were widespread attempts among Calvinist leaders to turn the family into a "little church."[3]

In North America in the twenty-first century, the very word "family" is politically controversial. Families come in many shapes and sizes, from extended households with aunts and cousins and grandparents, to single parents with children, to committed couples with no plans to have children at all. No longer does "family" mean a home in which the father operates as the pastor, guiding women and children in Scripture reading and prayer. Yet life in families, or in those close communities of relationship where we spend the majority of our time, continues to be a vital place to practice praying. Here too we need to hear Jesus' caution that prayer should not be for show. Yet prayer in close-knit communities can help us develop habits of thanksgiving, confession, intercession, and lament in ways that individual prayer alone cannot do.

A musical analogy can help us to think about how we pray in families. Music has components of melody, rhythm, and harmony—and so too does prayer life. By "melody" here I mean the fundamental tones that make up family or communal prayer. Think about the ways you pray in your own family: Do you primarily offer thanksgiving? Praise? Do you spend most of your prayers asking for help for others? Do you ever lament? (I will address all of these "modes of prayer" at greater length in the next chapter.) What makes up the basic melody of prayer in your household?

The rhythm of prayer returns us to the theme of the last chapter: As a family or close community, when do you pray? Morning and evening? Mealtime and bedtime? Spontaneously, as cries of lament in the car? What regular patterns of attention to God do you maintain, not only separately but together?

Harmony is a third basic component of music (at least in Western musical traditions): the juxtaposition of tones against one another to create a more complex sound. What does this have to do with family prayer? This is where we see most clearly the difference between individual and communal prayer: once "two or three are gathered," they will not offer prayers in identical fashion. And so our range of prayer is expanded by overhearing the thanksgivings and petitions of those at table with us. "I thank you, God, that I am six," says one. And though it is not my particular prayer, I can say, "Amen," giving thanks for the six-year-old to my right. "I pray for Tiger who is in heaven now," says another, and though I offer God a theological caveat that I do not pray for the dead, even beloved dead cats, I add this note of thanksgiving and lament to my own prayer. Harmony emerges in our nonidentical praying, and we each are enriched.

If we wanted to extend the analogy even further, we could explore how dissonance emerges in the context of family prayers, as it surely does also in public prayer. We could also think about the need for learning scales and basic chord progressions (fundamental musical patterns) in order to learn improvisation in prayer. But perhaps this brief exploration of melody, rhythm, and harmony is enough to make the point: prayer in families can shape us into communities who approach God together, and in doing so, learn to listen for God through the hearts and words of others.

Public Prayer

What do private prayer and family prayer have to do with prayer in public worship? In his discussion of prayer in the Reformation catechisms, Karl Barth points out that these teaching documents do not distinguish between private prayer and public prayer of the whole community. "One cannot ask whether it is the Christians who pray, or the church. There is no alternative, for when the Christians pray, it is the church; and when the church prays, it is the Christians. Between these two there can be no opposition."[4] Even more sharply, he says, "Although he prays for himself as an individual, [the Christian] does not pray private prayers."[5]

But wait a minute, you might be thinking. Jesus specifically said, "Whenever you pray, go into your room and shut the door and pray to your Father who is in secret." It sounds like Barth is directly contradicting Jesus. Jesus said only pray in private, while Barth is saying that Christians do not pray private prayers. How can we hold these two statements together?

Recall what I said earlier about the true and the false self. The false self imagines that it is independent, alone in the world, free to do whatever it wants to do. The true self, on the other hand, lives in communion with God. This distinction can help make sense of the apparent contradiction between Barth and Jesus. Jesus is teaching his followers that prayer is encounter between the true self and God, which is not what the "hypocrites" are doing when they pray loudly in front of others. In contrast to those who call attention to themselves in prayer, followers of Jesus the Christ are to pray with all their attention to God.

Barth, on the other hand, is addressing a different problem: the illusion of individualism. Modern people imagine that they are self-contained, self-directed, able to make private decisions without constraint by others. In contrast to this individualistic notion, Barth insists that Christians must not understand themselves as isolated. Rather, Christians know that our true humanity is bound up in Christ, which means that we are bound to one another. Therefore, when one prays, these prayers are not private but connected to Christ and to the prayers of the whole church.

There is deep connection between praying alone, praying in close communities, and praying with the whole gathered church. These three locations of prayer form a kind of "ecology" that shapes us into persons of regular prayer, an ecology to which we will return at the end of this chapter. But these are not the only places that Christians encounter prayer. What about praying in public, outside of Christian worship?

Praying in Public?

As a teenager, I attended a public high school in north Florida, where one of my greatest joys was singing in the choral program. In ninth-grade girls' chorus, and again as an eleventh-grader in the audition chorus, I was elected "chaplain." Mostly this meant that I was a kind of morale officer, giving a pep talk before each performance and addressing divisions among people when it interfered with our singing. The only nonnegotiable aspect of my job was praying with the group before each performance, concluding with the Lord's Prayer, which we all prayed together.

Looking back now, I have serious questions about those prayers. To be sure, most of us in chorus were Christian in some form, though we did have one Jewish soprano who sang all four years. No one was coerced into praying, whatever that might mean. And I conscientiously refrained from praying explicitly "in the name of Jesus" out of respect for the religious diversity of the group. Yet we were not a self-consciously religious community with common conceptions of the God whom we so blithely addressed before each concert. Apart from those prayers, we never discussed who God is and the nature of our relationship to the divine.

My colleague Mark Douglas has wrestled with the subject of public prayer in schools. In one editorial on the topic, he points out that "God does not come in a generic flavor."[6] That is, when we address

"God," we mean vastly different things, and our understandings of God are shaped by particular shared communal practices. For Christians, God is known most clearly in Jesus Christ, and therefore we share a paradoxical commitment to God who is Three and yet One. When we pray, we understand God to be simultaneously the one who hears our prayers, the one who prays with us, and the one who enables us to pray in the first place. This is simply not an understanding of God shared by our Jewish, Muslim, and Buddhist brothers and sisters.

Does this mean that Christians should never pray in the presence of people with other understandings of God? Not at all. But it does mean that we need to beware of two things in approaching public prayer: (1) we should not assume that we all mean the same thing by "God," and (2) we should not pray in order to draw attention to ourselves, but rather to draw our attention to the God whom we have come to know through Jesus Christ.

I have already mentioned the first danger: leading an assembly in prayer when that assembly does not share common faith in the triune God is *misleading*. Better to be honest about our differences and learn to pray near and for each other rather than glossing over religious differences in the illusion that we all mean the same thing when we address God. The second danger returns us to Jesus' words earlier in Matthew 6: "Do not be like the hypocrites; for they love to stand and pray in the synagogues and at the street corners, so that they may be seen by others" (Matt. 6:5). When we pray, wherever we pray, we need to remember the purpose of prayer: not to focus eyes on us, but to focus our own eyes on the triune God.

The Ecology of Prayer

Taken together, individual prayer, family or close communal prayer, and corporate prayer—and perhaps even prayer in public—form an ecology of prayer that in multiple ways turns our attention to God. When we pray "in secret," we do so knowing that this action calls us into community with others who similarly pray. When we pray in gathered worship services, we do so as particular people who encounter God in all the odd particularities of our individual lives. When we pray as families, we try to enter into prayer with our authentic selves oriented to God, and we also shape our little communities to better participate in the larger church communities with which we gather. If we pray in public, we pray not to some generic God, but to the same triune God whom we worship in Christian assemblies and to whom we turn in secret. These places of prayer do not oppose each other but can actually work together to draw us into habits of deep attention to the triune God in whom, to whom, and through whom we pray.

Questions for Discussion

1. Where do you pray most often: alone, with your family, or in corporate worship?
2. How does each of these contexts of prayer affect the others?
3. What makes a prayer both appropriate for use in public life outside the church and also faithful to Christian convictions?

Modes of Prayer

Be merciful to me, O God, be merciful to me,
*   for in you my soul takes refuge;*
in the shadow of your wings I will take refuge,
*   until the destroying storms pass by.*
I cry to God Most High,
*   to God who fulfills his purpose for me.*
* . . . .*
*   Awake, my soul!*
Awake, O harp and lyre!
*   I will awake the dawn.*
I will give thanks to you, O Lord, among the peoples;
*   I will sing praises to you among the nations.*
                                              —Psalm 57:1, 8–9

Writer Anne Lamott has said that she has two basic kinds of prayer: "Help me, help me, help me" and "Thank you, thank you, thank you." I am not certain where she learned these two prayers, but it could well have been from the Psalms. Though the Psalms include many different kinds of prayer, a common pattern begins with crying out to God for help in time of trouble and ends with praise and thanksgiving for God's help (or at least, for the promise of God's help).

Psalm 57 is a good example of this. The psalmist begins with the cry "Be merciful to me, O God, be merciful to me." Protect me in this time of persecution, God. Save me. The danger described is real: "I lie down among lions that greedily devour human prey; their teeth are spears and arrows, their tongues sharp swords" (v. 4). Help me, help me, help me. Yet suddenly the tone changes: "Be exalted, O God, above the heavens. Let your glory be over all the earth" (v. 5). And: "I will give thanks to you, O Lord, among the peoples; I will sing praises to you among the nations" (v. 9). From "help me" to "thank you" in a few short verses—this shows us that prayer does not always have the same basic tone but alternates between at least these two modes: asking for help and giving thanks for help received.

Chapters 6 and 7 addressed basic practical questions of prayer: *When* and *where* do we pray? In this chapter, we turn to another practical question: *How* do we pray? In other words, what is the appropriate tone to take when we come to God in prayer?

I suggested in the last chapter that in discussing prayer with families and close communities we think of it as having musical components of melody, rhythm, and harmony. Here we return to the idea of prayer as having "melody," that is, consisting of different tones that make up an overall offering of prayer. What basic tones make up your prayers? Do you mostly say, "Help me, help me, help me," or "Thank you, thank you, thank you"? Or are there other tones: "I'm sorry." "Help them." "Where are you?"

It has become common to refer to different modes of prayer in terms of the acronym ACTS (adoration, confession, thanksgiving, and supplication). To these, many recent scholars of prayer, informed by the Psalms, have added lament. This is an important but often neglected mode of prayer that we see in prayers such as Psalms 22 ("My God, my God, why have you forsaken me?") and 102 ("Hear my prayer, O LORD; let my cry come to you"). Together, these modes provide a basic five-finger exercise out of which we can construct melodies of prayer to the triune God.

Adoration

Awake, my soul! Awake, O harp and lyre! I will awake the dawn. . . . I will sing praises to you among the nations. This sort of prayer arises out of sheer wonder, sheer joy. In Psalm 57 it arises from joy at deliverance. Sometimes it comes as a gasp at the beauty of the natural world: "O LORD, how manifold are your works! In wisdom you have made them all; the earth is full of your creatures" (Ps. 104:24). Sometimes it is an exclamation of awe at the magnitude of God's greatness: "Praise the LORD! Praise the LORD from the heavens; praise him in the heights!" (Ps. 148:1). Always it comes with exclamation points.

Most worship services open with this mode of prayer. A prayer of adoration or a call to worship that summons people to praise emphasizes that God is both great and good: far beyond our comprehension and yet mysteriously benevolent to us. To go back to our discussion of the triune God in chapter 1, we might say that this mode of prayer attends particularly to God as the one whom we address, the transcendent One to whom our prayers are directed.

Confession

Beginning in "wonder, love, and praise," many worship services then shift their mode of prayer to confession. Having acknowledged the greatness and goodness of God, we become more aware of our distance from God, of our failure to live into the life for which God intended us. In chapter 2, I described this as the condition of sin, which names our situation as "not the way it is (or not the way *we are*) supposed to be." What do we do with this awareness?

Prayers of confession simply speak the truth about this condition in which we live: surrounded by powers that confine us, participating in actions that harm others and ourselves, seemingly unable to know or do the right thing. One traditional prayer offers this comprehensive confession:

> Merciful God,
> we confess that we have sinned against you
> in thought, word, and deed,
> by what we have done,
> and by what we have left undone.
> We have not loved you with our whole heart and mind
>   and strength.
> We have not loved our neighbors as ourselves.

Some hear this as depressing, as bad news, dwelling on the negative facets of life rather than the good news of the gospel. Yet recall that this is never the only form of prayer we offer; it is one tone of a larger melody that includes praise and thanksgiving. Furthermore, confession is not intended to make us wallow in guilt. Rather, confession names our situation of brokenness and complicity precisely in order that we can then hear the good news of forgiveness as genuinely good.

Recall Lisa Dahill's suggestion in the last chapter that in order to engage corporate prayers of confession more deeply, we might practice regular private confession as well. This enables us to acknowledge the specificity of our sin, to flesh out the general prayers about "what we have done and what we have left undone." Dietrich Bonhoeffer affirms this point in his description of confession in Christian community. We need to confess our specific sins, he says, in order to confront "the complete forlornness and corruption of human nature."[1] Real confession means acknowledgment of actual sin to God. It is not enough to repeat lovely words with the congregation on a Sunday morning; we need to admit the ways in which we specifically have harmed others, the world, and ourselves.

Furthermore, Bonhoeffer says, we need to do this not only alone and not only in community, but with another member of the Christian community. Bonhoeffer insists that "those who confess their sins in the presence of another Christian know that they are no longer alone with themselves; they experience the presence of God in the reality of the other. . . . When I come face to face with another Christian, the sin has to be brought to light." In other words, honest admission of sin before God and with another member of the community keeps us from self-deception and assures us of genuine community in God. In addition, "as the acknowledgement of my sins to another believer frees me from the grip of self-deception, so, too, the promise of forgiveness becomes fully certain to me only when it is spoken by another believer as God's command and in God's name."[2] We need to tell the unvarnished truth about ourselves to someone else who can then remind us of the unfathomable truth that God loves us anyway. The value of confession, and the reason it is indispensable in prayer, is that in confession we name the ways in which we are broken, so that we can receive the fullness of God's healing grace—both through the gospel message itself and through others.

Thanksgiving

Awake, my soul! Awake, O harp and lyre! I will awake the dawn. I will give thanks to you, O God, among the peoples; I will sing praises to you among the nations. Thus does the psalmist offer thanks following deliverance from the time of trouble—and so do we. Thanksgiving prayers recognize God as the source of all good gifts, including the large categories of creation and deliverance, as well as smaller, more particular gifts: gardenias, fresh chocolate chip cookies, a good joke.

Prayers of thanksgiving not only express our gratitude for such gifts; over time, such prayers can also shape us into fundamentally grateful people. The Heidelberg Catechism says that prayer is necessary "because it is the chief part of the gratitude which God requires of us, and because God will give his grace and Holy Spirit only to those who sincerely beseech him in prayer without ceasing, and who thank him for these gifts."[3] Does this mean that God waits for us to say "Thank you" before giving to us? Surely not. If the Scriptures tell us anything about the character of God, it is that God repeatedly reaches out to human creatures before we reach out at all: in providing the good earth on which to live, in calling Abram and Sarai (in Gen. 12), in drawing the infant Moses out of the water (in Exod. 2), and most clearly, in the person of Christ Jesus, who came to us "while we were yet sinners." God's care for us comes without prerequisites.

The structure of the Heidelberg Catechism itself underscores this pattern: the first section describes human misery, followed by a lengthy section about God's saving work that delivers us from misery. Only after these two sections do we reach the final portion of the catechism, which describes the Christian life of gratitude. The discussion of prayer occurs here. Clearly, God's grace precedes our gratitude. But Heidelberg's point is more subtle: we only come to recognize God's grace when we ask for it and give thanks for it. We only come to know it *as grace* when we acknowledge that these gifts are not things that we have earned or deserve. This is why the catechism says that God will give grace only to those who beseech and give thanks.

Does this sound counterintuitive? Think about how we actually learn gratitude growing up: writing thank you notes, being nudged by parents to say "Thank you" for gifts received, singing and saying prayers of thanks before meals. We do not know at first that all the things that come to us are gifts. We assume that the wrapped boxes and the food and the beauty around us are simply there. Why say thank you? But slowly, through the habit of giving thanks, we just might come to mean it. We just might come to realize that the world is filled with grace, from the hand of a gracious Giver. And so we say, with the Heidelberg Catechism and with Anne Lamott, "Thank you, thank you, thank you."

Supplication and Intercession

Be merciful to me, O God, be merciful to me, for in you my soul takes refuge; in the shadow of your wings I will take refuge, until the destroying storms pass by. "Help me, help me, help me." Here we turn to the corresponding tone of prayer, often paired with thanksgiving. Anne Lamott phrases it as a cry for help. Heidelberg calls it "beseeching." It is the form of prayer that asks for God's intervening grace, either for ourselves (supplication) or for others (intercession).

Here we face squarely the question: For what do we appropriately pray? Is it okay to pray for prosperity? For sports teams? For our side in a war? After all, Jesus said, "Whatever you ask for in prayer, believe that you have received it, and it will be yours" (Mark 11:24). Should we pray for parking places, or to find the right dress for a wedding reception?

Karl Barth says that prayer is simply asking, so all prayer is basically petition, or supplication. This seems to suggest that we simply follow Jesus' instruction to "ask, and the door shall be opened to you," no matter what the request. But Barth does not mean that prayer is simply asking for God to do stuff for us. Rather, asking is invocation, calling out to God to remind him that "he is [our] Father and [we] are his children."[4] Petition, according to Barth, points to a deeper relationship, even participation in God. In emphasizing prayer as petition, Barth is insisting that prayer is more than just talking to ourselves, and that God really does answer prayer.[5]

In chapter 4, I reflected on what it means to say that God answers prayer and noted two important things that relate to the theme of supplication and intercession. First, prayer itself is not something that we simply initiate; prayer is already our participation in the triune life of

God. Jesus Christ is already praying beside us. The Holy Spirit is already praying in and through us. If this is so, then when we come to ask something of God, we are not alone in asking.

Second, God does not always answer prayer in the way we expect, so just because we ask does not mean that God shows up like Santa with whatever was on our list. Responses to our pleas may come as judgment, or as deliverance on the far side of suffering, or as encounter with Christ in the midst of suffering. We ask for ourselves and for others not because prayer is a magic power that coerces God to do our bidding, but because when we pray, we are relying on a Holy Mystery beyond our own powers.

So it is appropriate to pray for ourselves and for others. When we pray in this way, we unite ourselves to the prayer of Jesus, lifting up the world before God. We do this not to invoke God's favor narrowly on a particular cause (this is the danger of praying only for our football team or only our side in a war). God is not our tribal deity to manipulate, but the Creator and Redeemer of the whole world. Rather, we pray for particular people and situations in order to place ourselves in God's hand, that we might discern God's ways in the world and live out these ways in our own lives. In interceding for others, we place ourselves attentively in the presence of God so that God might use us for the transformation of the world.

Lament

In the shadow of your wings I will take refuge, until the destroying storms pass by. I cry to God Most High, to God who fulfills his purpose for me. In adoration we cry out in wonder to God. In confession we acknowledge our distance from God. In thanksgiving we name the ways in which God surrounds us with grace, and in supplication we ask for our needs and for the needs of the world. Is this not enough? Not according to the Psalms. There are also times when life confronts us with such horror, or such tragedy, that we can only cry out to God in pain and anger. "I cry to God Most High," says the psalmist, or more poignantly in Psalm 22, "My God, my God, why have you forsaken me?"

It might seem impolite to address God in this way, but if we truly pray in and through Jesus, then we have a clear model for crying out to God in our anguish. Theologian Daniel Migliore puts this eloquently:

> Jesus is our representative, our great high priest, not only as the one who bears the consequences of our sins but also as one who laments on our behalf before God. He is the one who "in the days of his flesh . . . offered up prayers and supplications, with loud cries and tears, to the one who was able to save him from death" [Heb. 5:7].

That is, when we pray "in the name of Jesus" we not only intercede for the needs of the world, but we also lament our own pains and the pains of the world, as Jesus does. Migliore continues:

> Surely there has been an imbalance in many Christian theologies of prayer. . . . So little, if anything, has been said about the terrifying cry from the cross. . . . The prayer of lament safeguards the fact that our prayers are uttered in the shadow of the cross as well as in the Easter hope of the triumph of God's grace throughout the creation, and that consequently room must be made in our personal and corporate prayers for "the Friday voice of faith."[6]

Lament offers up the "Good Friday voice of faith," crying out in pain when we cannot give voice to thanksgiving or praise. Such honesty needs to be included in a full life of prayer.

Melody of Prayer

In chapter 2 we noticed the interplay of several elements of prayer in Psalm 42, reflecting some basic features of what it means to be human: We thank God for our lives—and we beseech God to come into those areas of our lives that are most God-forsaken. We thank God for sustaining the beauty of the world—and we beseech God to heal those areas in the world that are most God-forsaken. We cannot live apart from God—and yet we often live for long stretches without being able to sense God's presence. In this chapter I have expanded those tones and named them explicitly as adoration, confession, thanksgiving, supplication and intercession, and lament. How do we approach God in prayer? We do so in all of these ways, as we grow in our awareness of God's glory and grace, and in our reliance on the Holy Triune Mystery for our very lives.

Questions for Discussion

1. What tone of prayer do you use most often in prayer: adoration, confession, thanksgiving, supplication, intercession, or lament? Why?
2. What tone of prayer do you use least often? Why?
3. Is it appropriate to pray for parking spaces? If so, when and why?

Engaging All the Senses in Prayer

Then the prophet Miriam, Aaron's sister, took a tambourine in her hand; and all the women went out after her with tambourines and with dancing. And Miriam sang to them:
"Sing to the LORD, for he has triumphed gloriously;
horse and rider he has thrown into the sea."
          —Exodus 15:20–21

*S*o far, we have looked at prayer primarily as an activity that involves words, whether written or spoken, individual or corporate. But at this point we need to stop and ponder the question Dorothy Day once asked: "Since when are words the only acceptable form of prayer?"

In Exodus 15, Miriam dances and sings her praise to God for deliverance from the Red Sea. Shall we not call her actions a kind of prayer? In the last chapter we encountered adoration as the first tone of prayer, and surely this kind of prayer frequently expresses itself in joyful praise and movement, not just spoken words. In this chapter, we will consider briefly several ways in which prayer might involve more than just words, but the giving of our whole selves to God.

The Body and Prayer

Contemporary theologian Jürgen Moltmann claims that in the modern world we have lost the ability to see all of creation as alive and praising God: "All creatures are aflame with the present glory of the Lord, and reflect his glory in a thousand different mirrors, but 'we are blind, we have no eyes,' said Calvin, as did Francis of Assisi."[1] When we pray, we are simply waking up to the glory of God that is always already all around us. We are simply participating in the praise of God that is ongoing in the life of creation. Says Moltmann, "Prayer means coming awake. So praying also means awakening the senses."[2]

In the introduction, I offered several vignettes of prayer and suggested that in each case, a person or a group of people was "seeking or acknowledging or hoping for a dimension of reality more profound than their senses alone will admit." Prayer certainly drives us beyond our senses to acknowledge a depth of reality that is not limited to sense perception. Yet here we need to balance that earlier statement; though prayer presses us beyond our senses, we can only pray with the use of our senses. We do not pray as disembodied beings. And if we follow Moltmann, prayer is not just making use of our senses but fully engaging them, coming awake through sight, sound, and touch to God's activity in the world all around us.

For prayer to awaken our senses, it is helpful to pray with our whole bodies, not just our lips. Moltmann suggests that our very posture both reflects and shapes our prayer. Our bodies, in other words, have an effect on how we pray. He explores three sorts of prayer postures that reveal different ways of understanding and relating to God in prayer. First, he reflects on the practice of Muslim prostrations. What does this posture communicate? Subservience, absolute dependence on the power of God. But even more than this, Moltmann points out that this posture makes the pray-er "as small as possible; he is acting out his own insignificance and assuming the position of an embryo in its mother's womb."[3] There are parallels to this attitude in the Old and New Testaments as well: Abraham, Moses and Aaron, Joshua, Daniel, and the whole people of Israel fall on their faces before the Lord at various times, and the disciples fall on their faces before Jesus at his transfiguration. This bodily attitude communicates the absolute power and otherness of God in relation to humanity.

What about the prayer posture most common to Christians since the medieval era: kneeling, bowing the head, folding the hands, and closing the eyes? Moltmann points out that this too displays submission to God, acting out our unworthiness and our humility before our

Lord, much like subjects would kneel down and bow before their monarch. Again, we see allusions to kneeling and bowing down in the Christian Scriptures, as for instance in Philippians 2:10: "At the name of Jesus every knee should bend." Yet Moltmann cautions us that this posture turns the person inward, closing her off from the world around, shutting down the senses and seeking God only inwardly and in solitude.

Compare this with his description of a third posture of prayer, most common in the early church and depicted in the earliest Christian art in the catacombs of Rome and Naples. There, people pray with eyes open and arms outstretched, "the attitude of a great expectation and a loving readiness to receive and embrace."[4] This way of praying embodies the conviction that we are freed by God to give thanks and praise, to live as those fully awake. Orthodox priests adopt this posture when they pray for the coming of the Holy Spirit, and Pentecostal Christians also have adopted this attitude of prayer to express their joy and openness to God's presence. Moltmann calls us to this kind of prayer posture as the fullest expression of Christian freedom, for "people who pray like this are laying themselves open to the wind of the Holy Spirit, and are driven by the Spirit. That is incomparable freedom before God, with God, and above all *in* God."[5]

The main point here is that the way we use our bodies in prayer both communicates our understanding of prayer and shapes the way that we pray. Do we pray with eyes closed or downcast, bodies curved in, focusing attention on our humility? While this kind of praying has its place, you might experiment with Moltmann's third posture of prayer: eyes open, head up, arms out. How does it change your prayer? How does it shape your approach to God and your perception of your place in God's world?

Dancing?

Then the prophet Miriam, Aaron's sister, took a tambourine in her hand; and all the women went out after her with tambourines and with dancing. In celebration of God's deliverance, the women of Israel cannot keep still. Led by Miriam, they embody their praise in dancing. Nor is this the only time in Scripture that we see dancing as a form of praise. Psalm 149:3 calls, "Let them praise his name with dancing," and Psalm 150 echoes, "Praise him with tambourine and dance!" David notoriously danced before the ark of the Lord in celebration in 2 Samuel 6. Dancing embodies joy and praise for God's great works of deliverance.

In various times and places, Christians have danced before God as a form of prayer and praise. In eighteenth- and nineteenth-century America, for instance, a religious sect called the Shakers made dancing a central part of its worship life. With the accompaniment of songs such as "'Tis a Gift to be Simple," Shakers choreographed movements that contributed to their ecstatic prayer and praise. Today in Ghana, West Africa, men and women dance as they come forward to bring their offerings, embodying the joy of giving.

Yet many North American Christians share a history that regarded dance as something not of God. How could such a sensual, embodied activity possibly be a form of prayer? In *The Music Man*, traveling salesman Harold Hill plays on these fears when he addresses the folks in River City, Iowa, suggesting that the pool table that has recently come to town will lead inexorably to the dangers of dancing. "One fine night," he warns, "they leave the pool hall, headed for the dance at the armory! Libertine men and scarlet women and ragtime! Shameless music that will grab your son and your daughter with the arms of a jungle animal instinct! Mass hysteria!"[6] We got trouble, my friends, in River City or anywhere else where young people are grabbed by a "jungle animal instinct" in dancing.

To respond to this caution about dancing, let us return to the basic point introduced by Moltmann: prayer is awakening the senses. It is about engaging the body, whether we are aware of it or not. Our choice is not *whether* to involve the body in prayer, but *how*. We might kneel and bow our heads. We might fall on our faces before God. We might follow the example of early Christians and pray with heads lifted and arms outstretched. Perhaps we might even lift our heads, stretch out our arms—and move our feet!

At one congregation where I worship, there is a group that meets regularly for "full body prayer." They gather on Sunday afternoons, read and reflect on a passage of Scripture together, and then interpret that Scripture through movement. Some of these folks are trained dancers; others are not. The point is not professional quality performance, but expression of prayer through the whole body. At times they bring their interpretive movement into congregational worship, where it enables the prayer of the whole community. For those of us who sit in the congregation, such movement engages our eyes in a different way of praying. For those who dance, it engages their breath, their expressive faces, and every muscle in their bodies in praising God.

Breathing

Moltmann points out that standing upright with arms outstretched has one very specific effect on our bodies: it enables us to breathe more deeply, which produces the embodied experience of freedom and life. Yet Moltmann is not the only theologian to pay attention to breath in connection with prayer. In an earlier chapter, we encountered the Eastern Orthodox "Jesus Prayer," which consists of the words, "Lord Jesus Christ, Son of God, have mercy on me, a sinner." Manuals on this prayer pay close attention to how one is to breathe while reciting it. First, bow your head and lower your chin to your chest. Hold your breath briefly, and then begin praying the prayer slowly, drawing the breath in with the words "Lord Jesus Christ, Son of God," and exhaling on "have mercy on me, a sinner."[7] What is the effect of this? Orthodox writers describe it as drawing the soul back into the body, or turning the attention to the body's limits in prayer. Controlling the breath in this way also induces a state of calm and can produce warmth in the heart. Though this kind of prayer runs the risk of self-absorption, as Moltmann points out, it does share with Moltmann an intense awareness of the body and the way posture and breath have a profound effect on prayer.

Next time you pray, pay attention to what your body is doing. What does your posture suggest about your relationship to God and to the world around? How are you breathing? Are you awakening your senses and engaging in prayer with your entire body? Might you even find ways to pray through movement, through "full body prayer"?

Prayer and Visual Arts

If prayer is awakening the senses, then one of those senses that deserves our attention is sight. How do we engage our eyes in praying? Protestant Christians have raised serious concerns about praying with our eyes, because of the danger of idolatry. Indeed, in the sixteenth century, many Protestant reformers smashed visual symbols in churches, including images of saints, Mary, and even Jesus himself. In this, they were striving for a steadfast attention to God alone as the object of worship, abolishing any visible and tangible objects that might stand in the place of the Holy Trinity.

This caution about idolatry remains valid, Yet over four centuries after the sixteenth-century reformations, perhaps we need not be quite so leery of engaging our vision in prayer. The ecumenical Taizé community in France has exposed many Western Christians for the first time to the practice of praying with icons, a practice long central in the Eastern Orthodox traditions. A visual image of Jesus, or of Mary and Jesus, or of a biblical figure, rather than diverting our attention from God, can actually draw us more deeply into contemplation of God's works of salvation not apart from our bodies, but precisely in and through our bodies. Jesus was, after all, incarnate in a human body. Are we to deny our bodies, including our vision, in seeking God in prayer?

An old hymn begins, "Open my eyes, that I may see glimpses of truth thou hast for me." Another begins, "Be thou my vision, O Lord of my heart." Even Protestant Christians long for God to enable us to see rightly, to use our vision to see the world as God sees it. Icons or other images may be tools to focus our vision in this way.

Another way to engage our vision in prayer is through creating visual art, not just contemplating it. Painting, sculpting, drawing, work with ceramics or glass—all can draw our attention to God, not through words alone but through our hands and sight. Though I have no gifts in this area, I have friends for whom the creative process of making art deepens their attentiveness to God's creative energy in their lives. Even if, like me, you cringe at the idea of producing a piece of art that someone will actually look at, the process of drawing may itself enable a new kind of praying. In her book *Praying in Color*, Sybil MacBeth describes a simple process of drawing with abstract designs and words that focuses the attention, prompting more sustained, attentive prayer. She encourages people who find themselves distracted by trying to sit still and pray to take up markers or pens as aids to prayer. Though she addresses primarily intercessory prayer, her method can be adapted to other modes as well: thanksgiving, confession, or lament.[8]

Whether creating art or contemplating it, engaging the vision in prayer can help us focus our attention on one particular aspect of God's creation. It can also open us to the work of the Holy Spirit in and through us, as we ask God to be our vision and inform our own creative efforts. Either way, engaging our vision in the act of praying presents another avenue for offering our whole selves to God.

Silence

Thus far in this chapter we have explored various ways that we might engage our bodies in prayer: through different postures, breathing, dance, and the visual arts. In all of these ways, we awaken the senses, drawing our whole embodied selves into prayer. Yet focusing on all of these activities could lead to the impression that prayer has to be active, has to take the form of motion and visible expression. This could lead to an understanding of prayer as problematic as the misunderstanding that prayer always involves words. In saying that prayer involves the body, are we saying that we can therefore never be still?

Surely not. Recall Dorothy Day's words at the beginning of this chapter: "Since when are words the only acceptable form of prayer?" Her question draws us to attend to other embodied forms of prayer, as we have seen. But it also reminds us of prayer that involves no words at all. In other words, her words call us to the practice of silence.

Lisa Dahill also calls us to attend to the important role of silence, both in public worship and in personal prayer. In our culture, she observes, we fill our time with so much talk, music, and activity that we rarely stop and make time for authentic silence:

> I believe there is a reason for this wholesale withdrawal from the experience of silence in our society—much as we may lament its loss—and that it has to do with resistance to deeper levels of our

beings: unwanted feelings, intuitions, desires, or needs. . . . We are cut off from others, from ourselves, from God, from the earth, and this hurts so profoundly we can't bear to face it. To the extent we are resisting the One who shows up in our depths, we often run from silence as well. . . . Silence is not the most central practice of prayer and worship . . . but silence—authentic, terrifying emptiness—is a necessary condition for being able to receive [the gifts of Word and sacraments] in the first place.[9]

Dahill recommends that we spend regular time by ourselves in silent prayer to learn honesty about ourselves and receptivity to God.

The Taizé community in France has also helped many Western Christians rediscover the role of silence in public worship as well as personal prayer. If you have attended a prayer service in the Taizé tradition, you know how uncomfortable such silences can be at first. For several minutes after Scripture readings, the whole community sits together without speaking, without music, simply reflecting together on the words that have been spoken. For those of us driven by lists of tasks to accomplish, the first reaction to silence is anxiety: "What am I supposed to be thinking about? Am I doing it right?" And then the lists begin: "Okay, God, here are the things I know I am supposed to give thanks for. And here are the people I need to pray for." And maybe: "After worship, I really need to run to the store and get milk and orange juice." But gradually, with enough time, the silence just might seep in and begin to still the chatter. We just might, in the silence, learn to sit and wait for God to speak. By suspending the unending words that fill our ears, we can learn the difficult truth that Christ alone is "the one Word we need to trust and obey."[10]

Music

And Miriam sang to them: "Sing to the LORD, for he has triumphed gloriously; horse and rider he has thrown into the sea." While silence is a vital part of prayer, it should not be the goal of prayer. All of the embodied forms of prayer we have met in this chapter—posture, movement, breath, visual arts, silence—can draw our attention to the place of our bodies in prayer. If prayer is awakening the senses, then in many and varied ways we need to attend to all the senses when we pray.

Yet I have left for the end the form of embodied prayer that has from the beginning been at the center of Christian praying. Music, whether sung or played, seems to be an indispensable facet of worship and praise. Miriam's song is probably the oldest example in Scripture of such music making as a form of praise, and Miriam's words serve as a model for many songs that follow. In the book of Judges, Deborah picks up the theme, following Barak's triumph over the Canaanites: "To the LORD I will sing, I will make melody to the LORD, the God of Israel" (Judg. 5:3). The prophet Isaiah later recapitulates the theme when he foretells the return of the remnant from exile: "Sing praises to the LORD, for he has done gloriously. . . . Shout aloud and sing for joy, O royal Zion, for great in your midst is the Holy One of Israel" (Isa. 12:5–6). So too Jeremiah, Zephaniah, and Zechariah all call on the people to sing, celebrating the victory—or the anticipated victory—of God over all that would hurt or destroy.

The Psalms also offer clear testimony of the centrality of music in Israelite worship. They were themselves sung, and repeatedly they call on the people to "sing praises to the Lord" or "sing a new song to the Lord."[11] They also call on the people to play on harp, lyre, timbrel, organ—a vast orchestra of instruments. This emphasis on music has shaped both Jewish and Christian praying since the first century. In the New Testament we hear the evidence that Christian communities sang "psalms, hymns, and spiritual songs" as part of their worship (Eph. 5:19; Col. 3:16). The book of Revelation provides a vision of the faithful before the throne of God in the last days—and again they are "sing[ing] a new song" (Rev. 5:9; 14:3)!

Why has music played such an important role in Christian praying? To begin with, music engages our emotional lives more deeply than speech alone. When we are joyful, music helps us to express that more fully; when we are grieving, music gives clearer voice to that sorrow. Think about all of the instruments that the psalmist summons to make music to the Lord; speech alone is inadequate to praise the God who has delivered the people. Or at the other end of the emotional spectrum, think about the Thomas Dorsey song "Precious Lord, Take My Hand." Written after the tragic death of his wife and child, this musical prayer expresses anguish as well as the heartfelt hope that God will draw the singer out of the depths:

"Lead me on, help me stand; I am tired, I am weak, I am worn." With its slow chord progressions, this hymn not only expresses the pain of the composer but deepens the compassion of those who sing it, as the music rises and then falls to the final prayer, "Take my hand, precious Lord, lead me home." Music, whether sung, played, or heard, adds emotional depth to prayer.

Furthermore, music is deeply connected to memory. Teachers at all levels know this: if you can set a lesson to music, it will settle in students' memories more firmly, whether the lesson is the periodic table, Spanish vocabulary, or the fruits of the Spirit. So too with prayers: if we sing them, or hear them sung, they sink into our bodies in ways that do not soon fade. We wake up in the morning with songs inexplicably running through our heads. We hear a musical phrase in the background, and suddenly entire verses that we thought forgotten come to our lips. Older adults who are losing their capacity to think or speak clearly can often still pray through hymns learned in childhood. The power of music to evoke memory is another reason that it is such an important form of praying: it not only evokes emotion here and now, but it expands our storehouse of prayer for years to come.

Because of its emotional range and its profound connection to memory, music constitutes a most basic form of embodied praying, engaging not only the ears but the breath, the posture, and the entire body. As we sing with Miriam a song to the Lord, we may find that not only are we more attentive to the act of praying, but we are deepened in our very capacity for praise.

Engaging All the Senses in Prayer

Prayer, says Moltmann, means coming awake and awakening all the senses. In this chapter, we have explored a variety of ways to engage the senses in prayer: through posture, dance, breath, visual arts, silence, and music. Surely you will think of other ways to draw on all of the senses as you pray. The point is simply this: we are embodied creatures, and if we are to tune our whole selves to God in prayer, we have to take our bodies with us, not leave them behind. So join Miriam: take up your tambourine, lift up your voice, open your eyes, and present your whole self to God in prayer.

Questions for Discussion

1. What posture do you usually use for prayer? How does it affect your praying? How does it shape your approach to God and your perception of your place in God's world?
2. How do you use your eyes in prayer? Have you ever prayed by gazing at an image or making visual art?
3. How do you use your voice in prayer? Does music enhance or impede your ability to pray?

Prayer as the Chief Exercise of Faith

We do not know how to pray as we ought, but that very Spirit intercedes with sighs too deep for words. And God, who searches the heart, knows what is the mind of the Spirit, because the Spirit intercedes for the saints according to the will of God.

—Romans 8:26–27

What is prayer? This is the question with which we began. Throughout these chapters, I have described prayer as participation in the triune life of God. Beginning with the question "Who is the God to whom we pray?" we have explored together an understanding of God as mysteriously both One and Three— not only the one whom we address, but the one who enables us to pray and who accompanies us in prayer. In and through prayer, our true selves emerge, the selves who depend on God for our very being. Thus, we call out in thanksgiving and praise, in lament and beseeching, knowing that we rely for our initial creation and for every moment of our lives on the Holy Mystery that sustains us.

In this final chapter, I will suggest three ways of thinking about prayer that sum up what we have explored in the preceding chapters: prayer as conversation, as active receptivity, and as the "chief exercise of faith." Each of these images tries to name in a different way the paradox that is Christian praying: an act that is ours and yet not ours, and that occurs at certain times and places yet infuses every time and place of our lives.

Conversation with God

When asked to describe prayer, many Christians portray it as a conversation between a person and God. New Testament scholar Oscar Cullmann, for example, says, "The essence of all prayer is that it is a conversation with God as the partner."[1] He bases this observation particularly on his study of the Gospels. There, Jesus sharply criticizes all prayer that pretends to be conversation with God but is really not. For example, the Pharisee in Luke 18:11–12 prays, "God, I thank you that I am not like other people: thieves, rogues, adulterers, or even like this tax collector. I fast twice a week; I give a tenth of all my income." This address pretends to be prayer, but Jesus accuses the Pharisee of "exalting himself," focusing on his own merits rather than casting himself on God. This is not praying, but offering a monologue to God. In a conversation, however, people both speak and listen to the other. We do not only talk to ourselves. This is a crucial lesson about what it means to pray.

Prayer is surely a kind of conversation. As Cullmann points out, the kind of prayer that Jesus teaches is not simply talking out loud in order to draw attention to ourselves. It involves genuine give and take, genuine ability to attend to the other. This underscores the importance of silence, of listening, in prayer. We may have learned what we ought to say to God, but have we learned equally well how to attend to what God may have to say to us? The image of prayer as conversation helps us to see that praying involves real interaction, both speaking and listening to the Other.

If we think about prayer as conversation, we recognize that praying enacts a relationship. But this is not a relationship of equal parties; it is a relationship of creature to Creator. In chapter 2, I suggested that in prayer we acknowledge our dependence on God and realize our basic relationship to the One who gives us breath and life. The self we try to nurture in prayer is the true self, who acknowledges and delights in communion with God. So when we pray, we do not place ourselves on equal footing with God, but we place ourselves in the arms of the one who made us and sustains us at every moment.

Prayer may indeed be conversation of sorts, but this understanding of prayer has its limits. When we pray, we are not speaking to a visible person who responds in clear and straightforward tones. To be sure, I have met some people who have the gift of hearing the voice of God audibly, but even they tell me that this experience is not identical to having a human discussion. So whatever we mean by prayer as conversation, we do not mean that this is an exchange between two equal partners. When we hear God respond, it is more likely to be over time, in the depths of our being, or in a flash of insight, not an experience that is like the exchange with a friend across the table at the coffee shop.

The other problem with describing prayer simply as conversation is that it suggests two clearly separate partners, rather than the kind of complex relationship between us and the triune God that I have suggested so far. As Paul says in Romans, "We do not know how to pray as we ought, but that very Spirit intercedes with sighs too deep for words." In fact, we do not pray rightly by ourselves, but God's own Spirit enables us to pray. Better, therefore, to think of prayer as a conversation in, through, and with God, a relationship in which we speak to and listen for God but in which God also speaks through us. As I suggested in the first chapter, the wonder of prayer is that in the very act of praying itself, God is with us. God does not simply wait for us to get the words right before deigning to listen. The Holy Spirit inspires the prayers themselves, graciously leaning into our hearts so that God speaks to God through us. When we pray, we do not just enter into conversation with God; we enter into the conversation that is already happening within God's own heart.

Active Receptivity

We do not know how to pray as we ought, but that very Spirit intercedes with sighs too deep for words. Paul has already taught us that when we pray, we may be speaking to God, but God is also already speaking through us. This is the paradox I mentioned in chapter 3: prayer is simultaneously our action and not our action. Another way of describing this is that in prayer, we are both active and receptive, both putting forth our own effort and recognizing God at work in and through (and in spite of!) us.

As I have said repeatedly, prayer is not our triumphant ability to address God directly. It is the Holy Spirit's work in and through us. In this way, prayer itself is a gift of God. In prayer, we may speak, but eventually we realize that the words we offer are not even ours to begin with. They come to us from beyond ourselves. "Open our lips," we plead, and the words themselves confess that we do not open our lips or offer praise unless God first acts to enable our speech.

In prayer, we are already receptive to God's working in and through us. If we heed Jesus' warning and do not simply pray like the Pharisee in the temple, then we will not treat prayer as a celebration of ourselves but instead turn our attention to God. We might stop pouring out words to God and learn to listen and wait on God's word to us. When we pray, in other words, we learn to be receptive to the way prayer is not our action at all.

But does this mean that we are simply passive in this whole exchange? Not at all. As I mentioned in chapter 1, this is what Calvin was concerned about when he said, "These things are not said in order that we, favoring our own slothfulness, may give over the function of prayer to the Spirit of God, and vegetate in that carelessness to which we are all too prone."[2] To pray is not to vegetate in carelessness, but to open our lips regularly to proclaim God's praise—and thus hone our ability to see God as the one who has opened our lips to begin with.

Our earlier discussions about when and where and how to pray are relevant here. Regular praying teaches us how to listen more intently to God, but such listening skills require disciplined decisions on our part. Sometimes we have to turn away from the computer screen and the dishwasher in order to focus attention on giving thanks and offering intercessions for the day. This requires effort. Sometimes we have to program blocks of time in our schedules in order to pray. This requires effort. Sometimes we have to wrench our attention from the unfinished or ill-finished tasks before us to say to God, "I need your help," or "I am sorry, but I don't know what else to do." This can require a great deal of effort. So prayer is not just limp passivity but the activity of our truest selves as we come to rely more and more on God's life-giving Spirit.

Prayer as the Chief Exercise of Faith

The paradox of prayer as both ours and not ours is at the heart of John Calvin's discussion of prayer. He describes prayer as "the chief exercise of faith," our third and final image of prayer. The language of "exercise" suggests that there is an active dimension of prayer, that it is an endeavor that requires our attention and discipline in our daily lives. Indeed, Calvin himself says, "It is, therefore, by the benefit of prayer that we reach those riches which are laid up for us. . . . We dig up by prayer the treasures that were pointed out by the Lord's gospel, and which our faith has gazed upon."[3] It is not enough to sit back and acknowledge God from a distance. God is around, beneath, before, and beside us all the time, but if we never actively stop to notice this, to call out a breath of thanksgiving or petition, lament or praise, then we live falsely, pretending that we live as independent beings. Prayer requires our attention so that we might have our eyes opened to the way things really are.

Calvin insists on the importance of prayer, precisely because it shapes our perception so that we see rightly the relationship between God, the world, and ourselves. He lists six reasons why prayer is necessary:

> That our hearts may be fired with a zealous and burning desire ever to seek, love, and serve [God], while we become accustomed in every need to flee to him as a sacred anchor.
>
> That there may enter our hearts no desire and no wish at all of which we should be ashamed to make him a witness.
>
> That we be prepared to receive his benefits with true gratitude of heart and thanksgiving.
>
> That having obtained what we were seeking, and being convinced that he has answered our prayers, we should be led to meditate upon his kindness more ardently.
>
> That . . . we embrace with greater delight those things which we acknowledge to have been obtained by prayers.
>
> That use and experience may . . . confirm [God's] providence.[4]

Through regular prayer, Calvin says, we will learn to be grateful for God's goodness and rely ever more firmly on God's active presence in the world and in our lives. In other words, ironically, through the activity of prayer, we come to recognize ever more clearly that the truly active power in our lives is God.

This view of prayer is consistent with Calvin's understanding of faith itself. Go back to his definition of prayer: "the chief exercise of faith." So far we have focused on the word "exercise," noting the way this implies our active participation. Yet in order for us to understand Calvin's approach to prayer, we also have to pay attention to what he means by "faith." Faith, it turns out, does not grow out of our efforts. It is not exactly ours at all; it is the work of the Holy Spirit.

Here is Calvin's definition of faith: "a firm and certain knowledge of God's benevolence toward us, founded upon the truth of the freely given promise in Christ, both revealed to our minds and sealed upon our hearts through the Holy Spirit."[5] Do you notice the Trinitarian structure? Faith is knowledge of *God's* benevolence, based on the promise given in *Christ*, revealed and sealed by the *Holy Spirit*. Our faith turns us toward God's goodness, as we see most clearly revealed in Jesus Christ, and it comes as the result of the Spirit's work in our minds and hearts. So faith itself is a gift of the Spirit, a knowledge and trust that God's own Spirit instills in us.

What does this mean for prayer? It means that though prayer actively involves us, it does not begin with us. We are back to the paradox: prayer is both ours and not ours! If prayer is the "chief exercise of faith," then it is the activity by which God's Spirit works through us to draw us more and more closely into knowledge of God's goodness. This gives new meaning to Paul's statement that "the Spirit intercedes for the saints according to the will of God." In prayer, the Spirit (and not just we ourselves) is "exercising our faith," working to get our perceptions and affections in order so that we can see and live in the world properly.

Prayer and the Whole of Christian Life

What does it mean to see and live in the world properly? A full answer to this question would fill many books. Yet at the end of this book, let me say this much, and briefly: prayer in the end is not an isolated dimension of Christian life, but a basic attitude that shapes the whole of Christian living. Earlier I criticized the statement that "all of life is prayer," since that can lead to a total neglect of specific times of prayer in our lives. If all of life is prayer, I fear, none of life is truly prayer.

Yet there is a sense in which all of life should be characterized as prayer. Over time, with the Spirit's exercise, our inner selves can develop strong habits of attention to God's activity in our lives and in the world. The author of *The Jesus Prayer* describes a process by which praying the Jesus Prayer can lead one to see Jesus in everyone: "Under the faces of men and women we are able, with our eyes of faith and love, to see the face of the Lord. . . . If we see Jesus in everyone, if we say 'Jesus' over everyone, we will go through the world with a new vision and a new gift in our own heart."[6] This "transfigured" vision of all people in the image of Jesus affects how we treat others: not as enemies, but as beloved children of God.

Karl Barth describes the relationship of prayer and Christian living in another way. According to Barth, prayer is "the most intimate and effective form of Christian action. All other work . . . is Christian work . . . only to the extent that it derives from prayer, and that it has in prayer its true and original form."[7] This does not mean that prayer comes chronologically before work, but that "prayer is constitutive to all faithful Christian action."[8] Why does Barth say this? He believes that prayer enacts the basic relationship between humanity and God: our truest selves hidden in the life of the triune God. This is who we are, at the core of our being: beloved creatures, intended not for estrangement but for communion with God, filled with the life-giving Spirit, restored by the work of Christ, and set free to live in the world as if this were truly so.

St. Benedict gave his followers a motto that still guides the lives of Benedictine monastic communities to this day: *ora et labora*. Pray and work. This motto sums up the shape of good living for all Christians, within and outside monastic communities. Prayer does not draw us away from work, out of the world, but forms the basis for all the work that we do.

As you continue in your own life of praying, may it be the Lord who opens your lips, so that your mouth—and your entire life—may proclaim God's praise.

Questions for Discussion

1. Which of the images in this chapter is most helpful for you to describe prayer: conversation, active receptivity, or "chief exercise of faith"? Why?
2. Can you name a time when you were particularly aware of prayer being "not your action"?
3. Which of Calvin's six reasons for the necessity of prayer appeals to you the most? Why? Which do you find most difficult? Why?

Notes

Chapter 1: Who Is the God We Encounter in Prayer?

1. John Calvin, *Institutes of the Christian Religion*, ed. John T. McNeill, Library of Christian Classics (Philadelphia: Westminster Press, 1960), 3.20.5.
2. Westminster Shorter Catechism 7.001, in *Book of Confessions: Study Edition* (Louisville, KY: Geneva Press, 1996), 229.
3. See Dietrich Bonhoeffer, *Life Together and Prayerbook of the Bible*, vol. 5 of *Dietrich Bonhoeffer Works*, ed. Geffrey B. Kelly, trans. Daniel W. Bloesch and James H. Burtness (Minneapolis: Fortress Press, 1996), 54–55.
4. C. S. Lewis, *Mere Christianity* (New York: Touchstone, 1943), 143.

Chapter 2: Who Are We Who Pray?

1. See Perry LeFevre, *Modern Theologies of Prayer* (Chicago: Exploration Press, 1995), 118–19.
2. See Karl Rahner, *The Need and the Blessing of Prayer*, trans. Bruce W. Gillette (Collegeville, MN: Liturgical Press, 1997), 20.
3. C. S. Lewis, *Letters to Malcolm: Chiefly on Prayer* (New York: Harcourt, Brace & World, 1964), 82.
4. Karl Barth, *Prayer*, 50th anniversary ed., ed. Don E. Saliers (Louisville, KY: Westminster John Knox Press, 2002), 18.
5. For other examples of this pattern, see Pss. 22, 44, 74, and 83.
6. From the Great Thanksgiving for Easter in the *Book of Common Worship*, prepared by the Theology and Worship Ministry Unit for the Presbyterian Church (U.S.A.) (Louisville, KY: Westminster/John Knox Press, 1993), 318.

Chapter 3: What Then Is Prayer?

1. Karl Barth, *Church Dogmatics*, III/4, ed. G. W. Bromiley and T. F. Torrance (Edinburgh: T. & T. Clark, 1961), 97.

2. Karl Barth, *Prayer*, 50th anniversary ed., ed. Don E. Saliers (Louisville, KY: Westminster John Knox Press, 2002), 16.

3. Prayer in the *Book of Common Worship*, prepared by the Theology and Worship Ministry Unit for the Presbyterian Church (U.S.A.) (Louisville, KY: Westminster John Knox Press, 2003), 27.

Chapter 4: What Does Prayer Do?

1. C. S. Lewis, *Letters to Malcolm: Chiefly on Prayer* (New York: Harcourt, Brace & World, 1964), 69.

2. Heidelberg Catechism 4.129, in *Book of Confessions: Study Edition* (Louisville, KY: Geneva Press, 1996), 81.

3. Karl Barth, *Prayer*, 50th anniversary ed., ed. Don E. Saliers (Louisville, KY: Westminster John Knox Press, 2002), 13.

4. Todd Shy, review of *The Civil War as a Theological Crisis*, by Mark Noll, *Christian Century* (May 30, 2006): 34.

5. Fred Craddock, *Hebrews*, in vol. 12 of *The New Interpreters' Bible* (Nashville: Abingdon Press, 1998), 62.

6. David van Biema, "Mother Teresa's Crisis of Faith," *Time*, September 3, 2007, 42.

7. A Monk of the Eastern Church [Archimandrite Lev Gillet], *The Jesus Prayer* (Crestwood, NY: St. Vladimir's Seminary Press, 1997), 16.

8. Karl Rahner, *The Need and the Blessing of Prayer*, trans. Bruce W. Gillette (Collegeville, MN: Liturgical Press, 1997), 25.

Chapter 5: What Makes Prayer Christian?

1. Thomas Merton, *The Asian Journal of Thomas Merton* (1973), cited in *Thomas Merton: Spiritual Master*, ed. Lawrence Cunningham (New York: Paulist Press, 1992), 233.

2. A Monk of the Eastern Church [Archimandrite Lev Gillet], *The Jesus Prayer* (Crestwood, NY: St. Vladimir's Seminary Press, 1997), 27; Greek terms transliterated.

3. Ibid., 15.

4. Ibid., 40, quoting an early work called the *Centuries*, erroneously attributed to Hesychius.

5. Oscar Cullmann, *Prayer in the New Testament* (Minneapolis: Fortress Press, 1995), 102.

6. Ibid., 103.

7. Westminster Larger Catechism 7.290, in *Book of Confessions: Study Edition* (Louisville, KY: Geneva Press, 1996), 281.

8. Daniel Migliore, "Freedom to Pray: Karl Barth's Theology of Prayer," in *Prayer*, by Karl Barth, 50th anniversary ed., ed. Don E. Saliers (Louisville, KY: Westminster John Knox Press, 2002), 99.

Chapter 6: Times of Prayer

1. *The Rule of Saint Benedict*, trans. Anthony C. Meisel and M. L. del Mastro (Garden City, NY: Image Books, 1975), 66.
2. Karl Rahner, *The Need and the Blessing of Prayer*, trans. Bruce W. Gillette (Collegeville, MN: Liturgical Press, 1997), 39.
3. Ibid., 40.
4. Ibid., 42.
5. I thank Don McKim for this emphasis on the interplay of planned and spontaneous prayer.

Chapter 7: Contexts of Prayer

1. Lisa Dahill, *Truly Present: Practicing Prayer in the Liturgy* (Minneapolis: Augsburg Fortress, 2005), 9.
2. Ibid., 29.
3. Philip Benedict, *Christ's Churches Purely Reformed: A Social History of Calvinism* (New Haven, CT: Yale University Press, 2002), 511.
4. Karl Barth, *Prayer,* 50th anniversary ed., ed. Don E. Saliers (Louisville, KY: Westminster John Knox Press, 2002), 5.
5. Karl Barth, *Church Dogmatics*, III/3, ed. G. W. Bromiley and T. F. Torrance (Edinburgh: T. & T. Clark , 1960), 283.
6. Mark Douglas, "School Days, School Prays, Part III," *Sunday Paper*, August 26, 2007.

Chapter 8: Modes of Prayer

1. Dietrich Bonhoeffer, *Life Together and Prayerbook of the Bible*, vol. 5 of *Dietrich Bonhoeffer Works*, ed. Geffrey B. Kelly, trans. Daniel W. Bloesch and James H. Burtness (Minneapolis: Fortress Press, 1996), 113.
2. Ibid.
3. Heidelberg Catechism 4.116, in *Book of Confessions: Study Edition* (Louisville, KY: Geneva Press, 1996), 78.
4. Karl Barth, *Prayer*, 50th anniversary ed., ed. Don E. Saliers (Louisville, KY: Westminster John Knox Press, 2002), 78–79.
5. Ibid., 81.
6. Daniel Migliore, "Freedom to Pray: Karl Barth's Theology of Prayer," in Barth, *Prayer,* 113.

Chapter 9: Engaging All the Senses in Prayer

1. Jürgen Moltmann, "What Are We Doing When We Pray?" in *The Source of Life: The Holy Spirit and the Theology of Life* (Minneapolis: Fortress Press, 1997), 134.

2. Ibid.
3. Ibid., 126.
4. Ibid., 128.
5. Ibid., 129–30.
6. "Ya Got Trouble," from *The Music Man* by Meredith Willson (1957).
7. See A Monk of the Eastern Church [Archimandrite Lev Gillet], *The Jesus Prayer* (Crestwood, NY: St. Vladimir's Seminary Press, 1997), esp. 62, 68, and 107–9.
8. Sybil MacBeth, *Praying in Color: Drawing a New Path to God* (Brewster, MA: Paraclete Press, 2007).
9. Lisa Dahill, *Truly Present: Practicing Prayer in the Liturgy* (Minneapolis: Augsburg Fortress, 2005), 53.
10. Barmen Declaration 8.11, in *Book of Confessions: Study Edition* (Louisville, KY: Geneva Press, 1996), 311.
11. A good concordance can help you identify the many references to singing in the Psalms; a few examples are Pss. 9, 30, 47, 68, 96, 149, and 150.

Chapter 10: Prayer as the Chief Exercise of Faith

1. Oscar Cullmann, *Prayer in the New Testament* (Minneapolis: Fortress Press, 1995), 17.
2. John Calvin, *Institutes of the Christian Religion*, ed. John T. McNeill, Library of Christian Classics (Philadelphia: Westminster Press, 1960), 3.20.5.
3. Ibid., 3.20.2.
4. Ibid., 3.20.3.
5. Ibid., 3.2.7.
6. A Monk of the Eastern Church [Archimandrite Lev Gillet], *The Jesus Prayer* (Crestwood, NY: St. Vladimir's Seminary Press, 1997), 99.
7. Karl Barth, *Church Dogmatics*, III/3, ed. G. W. Bromiley and T. F. Torrance (Edinburgh: T. & T. Clark, 1960), 264.
8. Migliore, "Freedom to Pray: Karl Barth's Theology of Prayer," in Karl Barth, *Prayer,* 50th anniversary ed., ed. Don E. Saliers (Louisville, KY: Westminster John Knox Press, 2002), 101.

Further Reading

Barth, Karl. *Prayer*. 50th anniversary ed. Edited by Don E. Saliers from the translation of Sara F. Terrien. With essays by I. John Hesselink, Daniel L. Migliore, and Donald K. McKim. Louisville, KY: Westminster John Knox Press, 2002.

Calvin, John. *On Prayer: Conversation with God*. Louisville, KY: Westminster John Knox Press, 2006.

Cullmann, Oscar. *Prayer in the New Testament*. Translated by John Bowden. Overtures to Biblical Theology. Minneapolis: Fortress Press, 1995.